Charles Alden John Farrar

From Lake to Lake

Or, a trip across Country

Charles Alden John Farrar

From Lake to Lake
Or, a trip across Country

ISBN/EAN: 9783337077105

Printed in Europe, USA, Canada, Australia, Japan

Cover: Foto ©ninafisch / pixelio.de

More available books at **www.hansebooks.com**

FROM LAKE TO LAKE;

OR,

A TRIP ACROSS COUNTRY.

A NARRATIVE OF THE WILDS OF MAINE.

WITH THIRTY ILLUSTRATIONS, DRAWN BY REDER, GARRETT, REED, AND MYRICK.

BY

CAPT. CHARLES A. J. FARRAR,

AUTHOR OF "THE LAKE AND FOREST SERIES," "CAMP LIFE IN THE WILDERNESS," "THE ANDROSCOGGIN LAKES ILLUSTRATED," "MOOSEHEAD LAKE AND THE NORTH MAINE WILDERNESS ILLUSTRATED," ETC., ETC.

JAMAICA PLAIN, MASS.:
JAMAICA PUBLISHING CO.
1887.

PREFACE.

THE incidents that follow in these pages occurred during the year 1876, the first summer that a steamboat was ever run on the Richardson Lakes, and there have been marked improvements in the business of that region, also many changes in the places known to sportsmen and tourists at that time, in the intervening years.

The story is founded on the events that occurred during the author's first trip from the Richardsons to Parmachenee Lake, and it is hoped will please the general reader, as well as call to mind pleasant reminiscences to those more familiar with the country.

Should any of my readers ever make the trip from LAKE TO LAKE I sincerely hope that they may have better luck and better weather than I did.

CHARLES A. J. FARRAR.

ROCKVIEW, JAMAICA PLAIN, Feb. 1, 1887.

CONTENTS.

CHAPTER	PAGE
I. — We make a Start	13
II. — A Rough Passage	24
III. — A Night in the Woods	43
IV. — Killing Time	69
V. — A Sail on the Diamond	81
VI. — A Successful Hunt	93
VII. — Up the River	103
VIII. — Out of the Storm	129
IX. — A Quiet Sunday	145
X. — We Retrace Our Course	161
XI. — Bad News	181
XII. — The Wrecked Steamer	201

LIST OF ILLUSTRATIONS.

	PAGE
On Lake Molechunkamunk	Frontispiece
Jack tries the Trout	15
Aziscohos and Observatory Mountains	19
Whitney's Camp	22
Lake Molechunkamunk	25
Lake Welokennebacook	29
A Rough Passage	33
A Difficult Landing	37
Middle Dam Camp	41
A Diversity of Opinion	45
A Primitive Meal	49
Crossing the River	55
The Last Match	61
Duck-Shooting on Umbagog Lake	73
Through the Ice	79
A Lucky Shot	91
A Backwoods Residence	99
Crossing the Carry	105
A Cold Bite	113
In the Narrows	117
Through the Meadows	123
"Arctic Boating"	127
A Welcome Sight	133
In Camp	143
Homeward Bound	163
A Caribou Chase	169
A Road Accident	187
The Steamer as we found her	205
Righted up	209
In Port	219

FROM LAKE TO LAKE;

A TRIP ACROSS COUNTRY.

CHAPTER I.

*" There is a time to play ! 'Tis when
Our toil is o'er."* — EDDY.

WE MAKE A START.

OUR season had ended, and the jaunty little steamer "Welokennebacook," which had done such excellent service on the Richardson Lakes during the summer, was now securely moored at the mouth of the river, with her bow toward the rapids, while two large "driving" anchors from bow and stern held her in position. To make assurance doubly sure we had run a long, heavy cable from each side of the boat, amidship, to trees on either point that formed the little cove in which she lay.

After taking a last look around to satisfy ourselves that nothing remained to be done, we pulled to the landing, and drew the yawl carefully up on shore beyond the reach of any sea, and turning it bottom up covered it over with boards, that were held in position by heavy stones.

As we left the lake shore we took one more look at the gallant little craft floating at anchor, and a momentary feeling of sadness stole over me, as I thought of the pleasant hours I had passed on her deck that summer, and how seven long months must come and go before I should see her again.

Her deserted appearance also touched me. The flag-staffs had been taken down and housed, the smoke-stack and exhaust-pipe no longer appeared above the engine-room, and all the windows and doors had been covered with boards, as protection against the wind and hail and snow that were to buffet her through the winter.

"She looks as if the life had all gone out of her," remarked Jack, the engineer, who was with me.

"That is a fact," I replied. "Do you suppose she will stay there safely through the winter?"

"Why not? The ice won't freeze very thick there on account of the current."

"I was not thinking of the ice, but of the wind. There are such heavy blows here in winter."

"Oh, I guess she will be all right, Captain. But if we are going to get to camp before dark, we had better be moving."

Leaving the lake shore we struck into the road, and went up to the Upper Dam Camp, where we were stopping, and had our supper; and, as we intended to make

JACK TRIES THE TROUT.

an early start the next morning, we went to bed soon after eating. We had put in a hard day's work and we slept soundly. Indeed it seemed I had been in bed but an hour or two when I was awakened by the cook pounding on my door and telling me it was five o'clock.

Crushing the strong inclination I had to turn over and take another nap I arose quickly and dressed, and went out-doors to take a look at the weather. It bid fair to be a pleasant day, and as I turned to go in I descried Jack returning from the dam with a couple of nice trout. I waited for him to come along.

"Thought you would want trout for your last breakfast at the lakes, Captain, so I went down and snaked out a couple."

"What beauties!" I replied. "Where did you take them?"

"Down to the Apron. The two will weigh about seven pounds, I think."

We went into camp, took down the scales, and weighed the fish. One weighed three pounds and a half, the other four pounds.

The cook soon had them in the frying-pan, and at six o'clock we sat down to breakfast. As we did not expect to have anything more than a hasty lunch at noon we ate heartily.

We had picked up all our things the night before, and were ready to depart as soon as we arose from the table. I charged McCard to look after the steamer, and, bidding all the inmates of the camp good-by, we left just in time to escape an old shoe that the cook threw after us for luck.

We crossed the dam and went over to the lower landing, where we launched our boat and pulled down to Mosquito Brook.

It was a lovely morning, warm for October, and the lake was so smooth and calm that the foliage, with all its delicate leaves and twigs, and its gorgeous array of colors, was reflected with a mirror-like fidelity. The shadowy outlines of old Aziscohos and Observatory, two beautiful mountains that towered skyward north of us, were also thrown on the smooth water, a long distance from the shore.

"This is a jolly morning to start," said Jack, as our powerful strokes sent the light craft spinning through the water.

"It is simply perfect; if we have such weather as this all the way to Parmachenee our trip will be one of the things to be remembered."

Just then two loons bobbed their heads above water, not more than fifty feet behind us, and with taunting cries challenged us to make a target of them. This was too much for Jack, and he dropped his oar, seized his gun, and blazed away at them. The shot made the water boil all around them, but did no damage, and the birds, rising in the water, gave themselves a shake, and again sent forth their mocking notes, swimming about as unconcernedly as if there was not a gun within a thousand miles of them. Jack put in new charges

NORTHERLY VIEW FROM HEAD OF NARROWS.

and fired again, but with no better result. His success reminded me of the Irishman shooting the fox. Telling the story to a friend he said, "Bedad! the first toime I hit him I missed him; and the second toime I fired I hit him where I missed him before."

I remarked to Jack that we had better resume our rowing, for I doubted if he had ammunition enough in the boat to kill one loon, let alone two. We started onward again, a cry of triumph from the loons ringing in our ears.

"If we had not been in a hurry I would have fixed them," growled Jack.

An incredulous smile lit up my face, and I resisted the inclination to make game of my companion. He was something like a firebrand; it did not take much to set him into a blaze, and I did not care to begin our trip by stirring up ill-feeling. It is a very good thing sometimes if you know when to hold your tongue.

Off the half-way point we passed a flock of black ducks; but, as we were anxious to get to Whitney's Camp before Captain Cole went away, we did not stop to take a shot.

We ran our boat into the mouth of the brook and pulled it out on the sand, then went round to the back door of the camp. We stepped into the kitchen and found the captain just arising from the breakfast-table. We exchanged greetings, and then stated our business.

"Jack and I are going up to Parmachenee Lake by

the way of Lake Umbagog and the Magalloway, and we want you to go down to the Middle Dam with us and bring the boat back, and leave it at the Upper Dam. I will pay you for your trouble. Can you go?"

WHITNEY'S CAMP.

"Yes, I guess so. Can we pull four oars in the boat you came down in?"

"No, she only has one set of rowlocks."

"Then hadn't we better take a boat from here, and leave yours and to-morrow I will take it back to the dam?"

"Any way to suit yourself. Four oars are better for a six-mile pull than two."

"Well," said Captain Cole, "we'll take Harvey's boat then."

"She's an easy rowing boat," added Jack.

"So much the better," I said; and we waited the captain's pleasure.

CHAPTER II.

"The south wind blew,
And from its open mouth
Belched forth tremendous gusts
That waked the waters from their slumbers,
Dashing them into angry waves
That threatened all before them."

A ROUGH PASSAGE.

THE captain had arrived at an age where he had just as lief take things leisurely as to hurry, and it was fifteen minutes, or more, before he had put up his lunch, and lit his pipe, and then we went down to the boat-house and launched the boat. It was larger than ours, and I was glad to make the change, as it would not cramp us so much in rowing.

Our "collateral," as some of the lumbermen term their baggage, was transferred from the one we had come in, and in a few moments more we were afloat. Jack and I grasped the oars, a pair each, and the old captain, seating himself in the stern, took the paddle to steer with.

The lake was still smooth, and the rising sun had

North-West View of Lake Molechunkamunk.

taken the sharpness out of the air, so that we soon found it warm work rowing. After passing Ship Island we took off our coats and vests, and settled down to business.

Reaching Metalluc Point, we rested on our oars for a few moments to catch a last glimpse of the lovely lake that lay bathed in the beauty of an autumnal sunlight, fringed with a border of reflected colors from the magnificent forests that swept back from its shores. Then, dipping a cup into the pure nectar on which we floated, we appeased our thirst, and again bent to our oars.

"I'd like ter have some o' them city fellers who come down here fishin' see the lake this mornin'," puffed Captain Cole between the whiffs of his pipe; "it's as purty as a picter."

"You're right," chimed in Jack; "it's a handsome sight."

We passed swiftly through the Narrows, and as we reached the lower end we began to feel a freshening breeze.

"Guess there's a purty good south wind on the lower lake," said Captain Cole, as he squinted in that direction.

"Yes, and some sea with it," I replied, as our boat, shooting around Portland Point, began to pitch into it, and send the spray in a shower over the bow.

"I'll be hanged if the lake isn't white!" exclaimed Jack, as he took a look over his shoulder, and noticed the long rollers curling gracefully over, and sending a sheet of white foam before them.

"Let me row now," said Captain Cole; "I'm gettin' a leetle stiff handling this ere paddle."

"Well, you can change with Jack," I suggested.

"No, sir," replied Jack; "I had rather row than steer, and, besides, we need a good hand at the wheel, — paddle, I mean, — for it will be confounded rough before we get over to the Middle Dam."

I accordingly changed seats with Captain Cole, and Spot followed me. Spot was a Scotch terrier who had been at the lakes with me all summer, and who enjoyed boating and tramping in the woods fully as well as his master.

Jack pulled the bow oars, and he held the boat up to the wind while the captain and I changed places, or attempted to do so.

As I arose to my feet an enormous roller struck the boat broadside on, and carried her up skyward. I lost my balance, and as our craft swept down in the trough of the sea I went out into the angry waters of the lake in anything but a dignified manner.

I was not hurt any, although the boat drifted over the hole I had made in the lake, but I was very disagreeably surprised. The first thought that occurred to me, as the waters closed over my head, was the fact that I could not swim a stroke, and I wondered how far the boat would be from me when I arose to the surface.

Down, down, down I went, in my excited state I

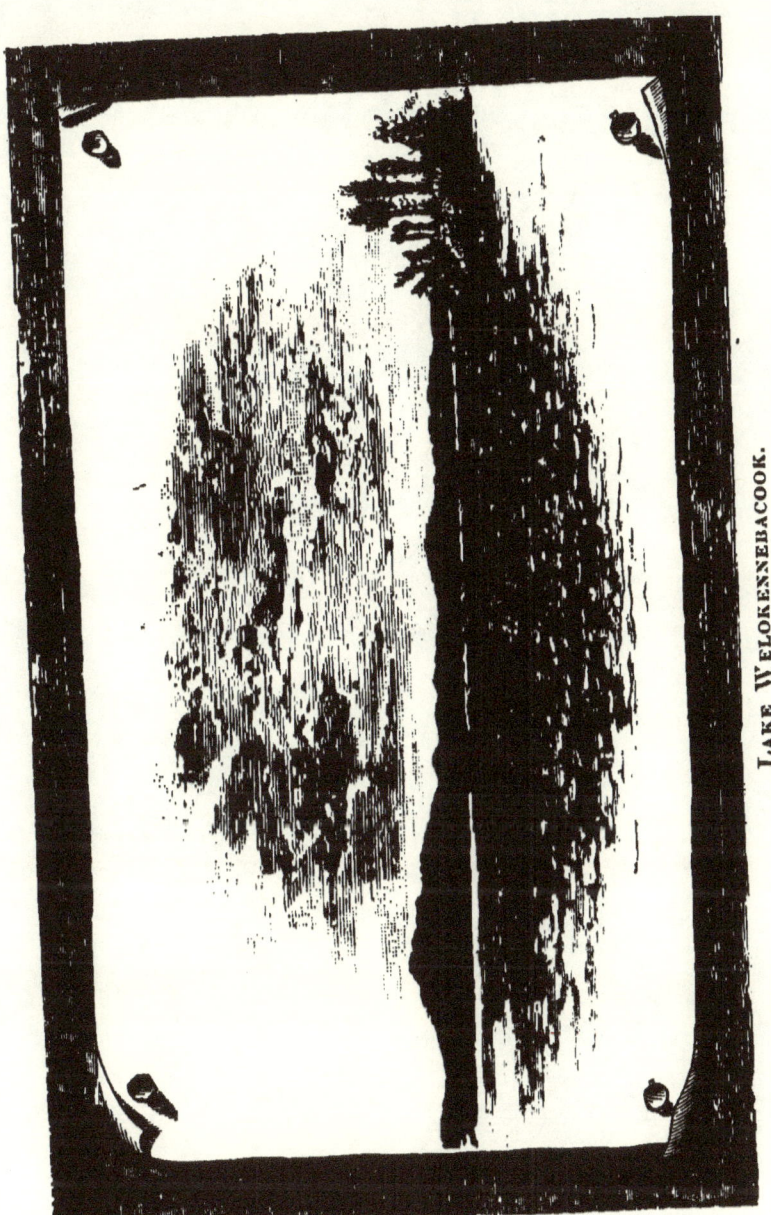

Lake Welokennebacook.

thought a mile or more; but, with a due regard for truth, I am willing to take off a few feet. Scientific men may say that drowning is an easy death. I deny it. I wonder if they were ever half-drowned before they gave their opinion. The ringing in my ears, the pressure on my head, and the choking sensation in my throat before I thought of closing my mouth, were perfectly awful. I never shall forget them while I live. To add to this the water was as cold as ice, and, with all my clothing on, I seemed to weigh a ton. I cannot seem to remember when I began to rise, but I opened my eyes just as my head came above water, and saw the boat about ten feet from me. My cap had gone adrift, and I shook my head to clear the water from my eyes, and sang out "Boat ahoy!" to the top of my voice, and then tried to swim. My experiments in this line were decided failures, and I should certainly have sank the second time had not Jack and the captain been on the lookout for me, and pulled toward me the moment my head appeared above water. In spite of all my efforts I was gradually going down again, when the bow of the boat came within my reach, and, making a last desperate plunge, I succeeded in grasping the gunwale of the boat in my left hand.

The moment I had a good grip on the boat I was as cool as a girl is to her lover when he is chanting the praises of her rival. Telling the captain and Jack to be careful that the boat did not upset, I worked my way along to the stern, and then, with the captain's aid, climbed in.

"By gracious, Captain!" exclaimed Jack, "you gave me an awful shock! I knew you could not swim, and I was afraid you would be drowned."

"A man who is born to be hanged, you know," I replied, with a poor attempt at a joke; but my teeth chattered so that I could not finish the sentence, and I settled back in the stern seat, and picked up the paddle.

"Did ye swaller much water?" queried Captain Cole.

"Enough to last me all winter; and now give way, for I shall freeze if I don't take some exercise."

I have never drank a drop of spirituous liquors in my life, to my remembrance; but if a flask of whiskey had been among the "ship's stores" about the time that I came out of the lake I believe I should have been strongly tempted to have seen what virtue, if any, there was in a good square drink.

As the captain and Jack gave way I dipped the paddle into the water, and headed for the sand-beach above the old Middle Dam Camp.

And now commenced a struggle with wind and wave that was anything but child's play. The wind steadily increased in power, and the waves in size, until it was all we could do to make the least head-way. As the huge rollers bore down upon us, threatening to engulf us, I would luff a little so that the boat would ride the wave quartering; but still I could not prevent our

A Rough Passage.

A ROUGH PASSAGE.

getting thoroughly drenched with spray, and quite a body of water would occasionally come into the boat, making bailing fully as important a business as steering. Between the two I had my hands full, and Spot, who had received two or three duckings, crawled behind my legs for protection. I was sorry to have my companions get wet, but the showers of spray were nothing to me after my bath in the lake.

"Well, this is a leetle rough'n I ever saw it on this lake," bawled Captain Cole, for it was impossible to make each other hear unless we yelled at the top of our voices.

"It's as rough as I want to see it, and a good deal wetter," howled Jack, as a big roller struck on the port bow of the boat and deluged him with spray.

"We are right in the worst of it," I exclaimed, for we were now opposite Jackson Point, which was on our starboard quarter, and we were exposed to the full fury of the wind as it swept up from the South Arm.

It was not a time for much talking, and I paddled and bailed alternately for dear life, while my two companions bent to the oars with a will.

"You're a good Samaritan, Captain," grinned Jack, as he watched my efforts to free the boat of water.

"Why?" I questioned, not seeing the force of his remark.

"Because you are going bail for us;" and he winked his left eye, and opened his mouth wide enough to have swallowed a country flapjack.

"You ought to have six months for that," I asserted, and then I let the boat fall off a little and catch a wave just right to give him a good ducking.

"Confound you!" roared Jack, spitting the water from his mouth; "you did that purposely."

I put on my most innocent look, and shook my head, but I could see that Jack doubted me.

Little by little we gained on our landing. One minute the boat high up on the top of a roller, the next in the bottom of a gulf, with a wall of water on each side that we could not see over.

I had crossed the lake a great many times, but never had I seen a harder wind or rougher sea than this, and I felt thankful when, after an hour's hard work, we had got within a few rods of the shore.

We found the waves rolling up on the beach ahead of us in a manner that threatened to capsize the boat if we were not careful in making a landing.

"What do you think of it, Captain?" asked Jack, who had been inspecting the shore over his shoulder. "I don't think we can be any wetter than we are now," I replied; "so let's go in on the top of a wave and the moment the boat touches bottom jump over the side and run her up out of the way of the surf before she has time to fill, as she certainly will if we are not quick."

We steadied the boat on the water a few fathoms from shore, and in a moment there came a tremendous roller, that lifted our craft and shot her ahead like an

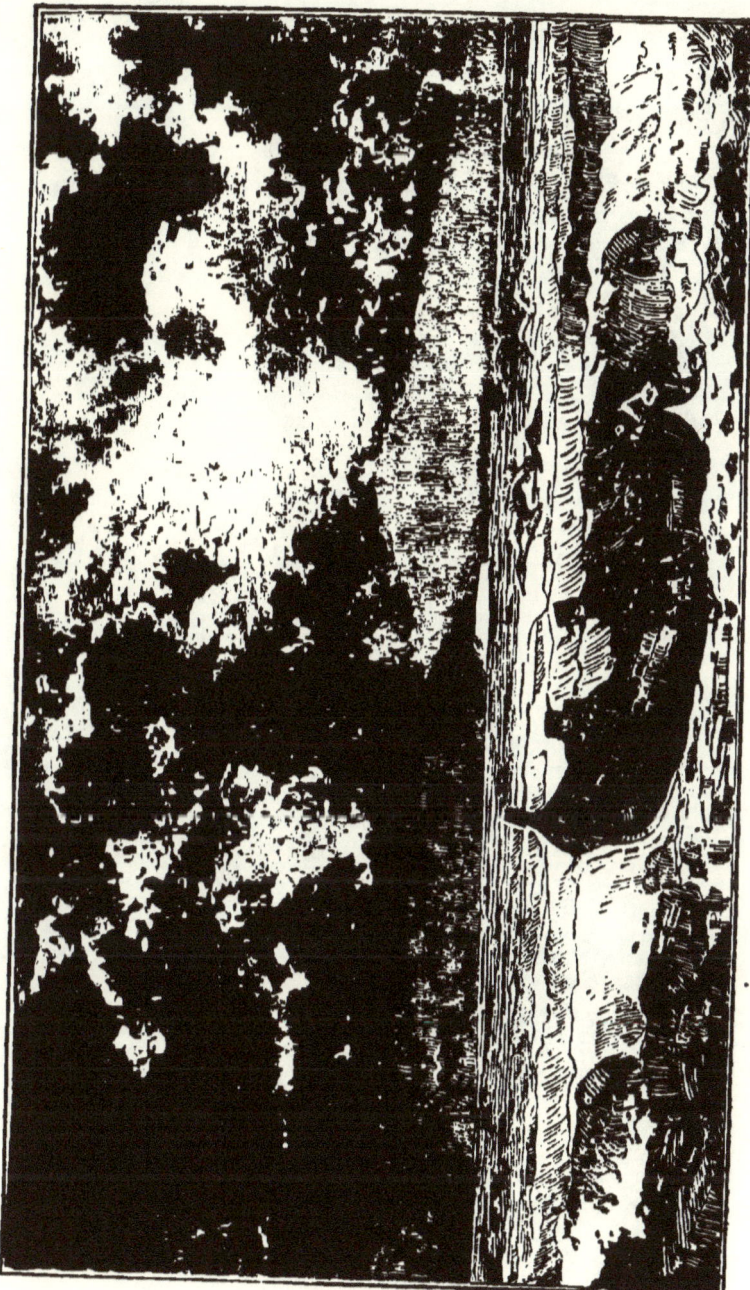

A Difficult Landing.

arrow. "In oars!" I cried, and as I felt the first touch of her keel I yelled "Jump!" and, suiting the action to the word, over we went, the dog following us, and, catching hold of the boat by the gunwales, ran her high and dry before a wave could break into her.

"That was a lively pull, that last two miles," said Jack, as he picked up his gun, and emptied the water out of the barrels.

"A little exciting," I returned; "but suppose we take our things up to camp."

Our luggage was light, as I had sent all my baggage and better clothing out to Andover the week before. We had with us a double-barrelled gun, a Smith & Wesson seven-shooter, a supply of ammunition, a drinking-cup, matches, a luncheon, a dull axe, a game-bag, and our overcoats.

I had suggested to Jack the advisability of grinding our axe before we left the Upper Dam, but he thought we would not need to use it until we reached Upton, and could do it there,— a neglect that caused us some trouble that night.

We deposited our things on the piazza, and then tried the different doors of the camp to see if anybody was there. But the house was empty, and the doors were all fastened. So we stripped without further delay, rung the water out of our clothing, then put it on, and ate our luncheon, or rather that part of it that had not been destroyed by the water washing into the boat.

"How do ye feel now, Cap'n? Have ye got warmed up?" queried Captain Cole, as he joined us on the piazza.

"Oh, yes; I am all right now, thank you, and none the worse I hope for my bath."

"Wall, if yer don't get cold yer all right. But I tell ye, I felt frightened when ye went over into that big sea; I snum I did."

"Shall you go directly back, Captain Cole?" I asked.

"Not while it blows the way it does now," he returned, smiling, as he puffed away at his pipe; "this wind will go down some by three o'clock, and then I can crawl out by the p'int, and get a little lee, then head nearly straight up the lake. I tell you a boat would make bad weather of it out there now;" and the captain glanced across the lake with eyes that were open to its perils.

"Then we shall have to leave you, for it is quite a tramp from here to Upton, and we want to get through the woods before dark. Take this for your trouble," and I handed him a bill. "I hope you will get back all right."

"Don't worry about me. Good luck to you," he said, as we shook hands and left him; "hope you will fetch Upton before dark."

Middle Dam Camp, Lake Welokennebacook. (1876.)

CHAPTER III.

"Cease to lament for that thou canst not help,
And study help for that which thou lament'st." — SHAKSPERE.

A NIGHT IN THE WOODS.

AS near as I could figure we were about nine miles from our objective point for the night, and, as the greater part of the way lay through the woods, over a road that had not been used much for years, and was quite difficult to follow, it behooved us not to loiter. An additional reason, if any were needed, was the fact that neither Jack nor I had been over the route we were to travel, and only knew about it from hearsay. But as yet I did not apprehend any difficulty or delay, although I knew we had to cross the river. Taking our overcoats on our arm we started on a brisk walk down the old carry road. Jack was pulling at his pipe, and that reminded me that I had some cigars in my overcoat. They were in an inside pocket, and, fortunately, had not been wet. In a moment I had applied the light of a match to one of the weeds, and was puffing along beside him.

"Twelve o'clock," said Jack, as he looked at his watch; "how far is it to Upton?"

"About ten miles, and, as we don't know the road very well, we have no more time than we want."

We scared up several flocks of partridges on our way, but did not get a shot at any of them. Just beyond Forest Lodge we stopped to get a drink, and for the first time noticed that the sky was becoming overcast.

"It looks as if we might get a storm to-night, Captain," said Jack, as he took a look around at the clouds.

"Then let's be moving forward," I replied; "we don't wish to spend the night in the woods. Come, Spot;" and I started along.

"It would be a nice joke if we had to camp out to-night. No grub and not a blanket between us, eh, Captain?"

"Yes, too much of a joke. But I expect to sleep at Upton to-night, don't you?"

"Of course. And if we don't we shall lose the boat. You know to-morrow is Tuesday, and she will go up the Magalloway."

"Yes, and if we miss her we shall have to stay at Upton until Friday, for at this season of the year she does not make that Magalloway trip but twice a week."

"That is so," replied my companion, "and we must reach Upton to-night."

A DIVERSITY OF OPINION.

About two o'clock we came to a point where the road forked, and we could not agree which road to follow. I wanted to take the left-hand one, and Jack the right. I had been over the carry as far as the cedar stump several years before, and was quite sure that the left-hand road was the one we should travel. On the contrary, Jack insisted that we should follow the one to the right, and, as I could not agree with him, we did as juries do in similar cases, — agreed to disagree.

It seemed a foolish thing to do, this parting company in the wilderness under the circumstances in which we were placed; but Jack was stubborn and was bound to have his own way, and as I had the advantage of having crossed the carry once, while this was his first attempt, I could not conscientiously follow him. I had an inward conviction that my choice of roads was the right one, and did not care to put in several miles of extra walking just to gratify his whim. Before we parted I made a last effort to coax him to accompany me, but it was only so much time wasted.

Each one now took the things that belonged to him, and, wishing each other good luck and a pleasant journey, pursued our separate ways.

Whistling to Spot I started down the left-hand road, and in a moment had lost sight of my companion. A few minutes' walk satisfied me that I was right, as I began to recognize objects along my way.

Shortly after leaving Jack the dog raised a flock

of partridges, and I was lucky enough to shoot one with my revolver. Taking the bird by the legs I carried it along, and after some fifteen minutes' walk from the main road I reached the river landing known as the Cedar Stump, and knew that I was all right thus far. Then I fired three or four shots from my revolver to let Jack know I had found the place, a signal agreed on when we parted.

We had expected to find a boat here to cross the river in; but, to my surprise and alarm, nothing in the shape of a boat was to be seen. Knowing that the owners of boats in that section of the country sometimes hid them when not in use, I began a diligent search along the bank of the river, both above and below the building, in every hole or corner that offered the slightest chance of concealment for a boat. But in vain I searched. Not a water craft of any shape was to be found, and, tired and discouraged, I returned to the landing.

We are in a nice pickle now, I thought, — no boat, and on the wrong side of the river. I see no way of getting across unless we build a raft; for the river was deep and quite wide, with an angry current that forbade swimming or fording. However I took the matter easily, for I had been in the woods too much to let any slight accident disconcert me. I began to feel hungry, so started a fire.

When it was well under way I took my partridge and, after plucking it, cut it open, then went down to

A PRIMITIVE MEAL.

the river and cleaned it. Then I took a long green stick, and running it through the bird held it over the fire until it was roasted, Spot sitting by and watching the cooking with a watering mouth.

I had put a small paper of salt in my vest-pocket on leaving camp in the morning, in anticipation of shooting a partridge, and drawing it forth I sprinkled some on my "chicken," and made a hearty meal, throwing the remains to the dog.

As I arose to get a drink of water I heard the report of a gun some way below me, and, thinking it must be Jack, answered it with my revolver. In about fifteen minutes I heard another report, nearer this time, and again I answered, and shortly after I descried Jack on the bank of the river coming toward me.

I began now to look around to see what material we could find for a raft; but the prospect was not very encouraging. I found on the bank above me a couple of dry cedars, about twenty feet long, and, rolling them into the river, floated them down to the landing, and pulled an end of each up on shore, so that they could not float away. By this time Jack had reached the landing; he looked tired and sheepish. He had a couple of partridges with him that he had shot down the river.

"Well, my boy," I said, "you have not been to Upton yet."

"No; the road I followed ended at the lake. Then I struck off through the woods to the left and found the river, and followed it up to this point. But let's go across, the afternoon is slipping away fast."

"That is easier said than done," I replied; "there is no boat here."

"No boat!" and my companion's eyes opened wide with astonishment.

"No boat," I chuckled, for I had recovered from the first feeling of alarm, and began to look upon our fix as a good joke.

"I thought Godwin always kept one here."

"If he did they must have taken it away the day they broke camp, for I have hunted high and low, and can't even find the ghost of one."

"This is a nice scrape to be in," he replied, with a tone of alarm: "perhaps you have overlooked it."

"Well, if you can find it you will do better than I can; and, as I suppose you will not be satisfied until you look, you had better do so at once, and I will keep at work raising the material for a raft."

"A raft!" he exclaimed, contemptuously; "how are you going to make a raft without hammer, saw, or nails, and an axe with a blade like a handsaw?"

"That is the question," I replied; "but it has got to be done all the same, and just bear in mind that if you had listened to me we should have had a sharp axe."

Jack turned away, unable to deny my assertion, and began hunting through the underbrush for the boat that was not there, while I continued to get together

A NIGHT IN THE WOODS. 53

anything and everything that would float, that I could lay my hands on.

About the time he gave up hunting for the boat I had completed my collection, and a queer-looking pile it made. Small logs and poles, stumps, a few boards and stray planks, and a couple of young spruces I had managed to hack down with the axe.

Out of the boards and planks I had been fortunate enough to get about twenty nails, and these, with some green withes, and about thirty feet of strong marline, were all we had to fasten our craft together.

As soon as Jack was convinced that there was no boat to be found he took hold with alacrity to help me build the raft.

We used our four largest and driest logs for the bottom and nailed the two planks across them. Then we put the three remaining logs on top of the planks, and bound them down as securely as we could with the marline and withes. We filled the spaces between the logs with light, dry poles, taken from a deserted river-driver's camp near us, and then nailed on our four boards for an upper deck. On top of these we rolled two or three dry pine stumps, getting them all together in the middle, forming a place to stand on that was about a foot above the floor of the raft. Then we brought down a couple more of the longest and lightest poles we could find around the river-driver's camp, to propel our ungainly craft with.

"Now where shall we land on the other side?"

asked Jack, who was scanning the opposite shore for a desirable point.

"That little cove is just the place," I answered, nodding toward a miniature bay a few rods below us, on the other bank of the river.

"I am afraid the current will sweep us by it if we start from here," and Jack calculated the distance.

I threw a stick into the river and watched it as it floated down, and then felt sure his supposition was correct.

"You are right, my boy; we shall have to start from higher up the stream; but let's get the old craft into the water, and see how she floats."

Carefully we launched the raft upon which so much depended, and taking our poles stepped on, the dog following us. The old craft settled down until the water was even with the upper deck.

"By Jove! this is a pretty ticklish affair, Captain. I don't believe we can cross on it and take our things at the same time; every pound will count."

"If there was any way of getting it back you might go over alone," I returned.

"I think it would float you and I and the dog, if we had nothing else, and I'll tell you what I think we had better do. You take off your coat and give it to me; with our overcoats, my gun and the ammunition, game-bag, and those big rubber boots of yours, I will try and get to the other side. If I succeed I will leave the things and then come back for you and the dog."

CROSSING THE RIVER.

"Spot can swim. You and I together will be all the old craft will carry."

We accordingly put all the things on the raft, and I kept it off the shore while Jack poled it up stream a short distance.

"Now give her a push," he said, "and we will see what she will do."

I gave him a send off and he began to float down stream.

"If the old thing comes to pieces in the middle of the river, throw me a life-preserver, will you?" and Jack laughed.

"Two or three," I replied; "life-preservers are very plenty about here."

He managed the clumsy craft well, and succeeded in making the cove. He took off the things, pulled off his coat and boots, and laid them on shore, and then started to return.

"Head up stream pretty well, Jack," I yelled.

"All right," he answered, and plied his pole diligently.

Spot and I watched him anxiously, but he reached us in safety.

"Come on, Captain," he cried, "for the sooner we are over the better; it begins to grow colder and looks more like a storm."

I did not need any urging.

As the raft struck the shore I jumped on, and took my seat on a stump, Jack declaring he could manage the craft alone. The dog followed, and I was about to pitch him into the river, when Jack interfered for him, saying the raft would carry us all. It did, after a fashion; but I was not sorry when it grounded in the little cove, and we sprung on shore.

We put on our boots and coats, and, taking the rest of the things in the most convenient way we could carry them, struck off down the river.

It was five o'clock when we left the raft; the sun had been clouded in for a couple of hours, and it began to feel like snow. But the exertion of walking kept us warm, and we made our way along as fast as possible.

It was the worst piece of country I had ever traveled over. The ground was uneven and rocky, and in some places we could scarcely force our way through the underbrush. We often came to clumps of windfalls, piled up in such a manner as nearly to stop our progress; but, by climbing over some and crawling under others, we managed to make slow headway. Occasionally we struck a bayou that made in from the river, and we were obliged to make long detours to clear them. Finally, after an hour's hard work, we reached the old Magalloway bridge piers just at dusk.

From this point it was six miles to Upton by an old road that had been discontinued many years, and consequently was none too plain to follow, especially in the night. We rested at this spot a few moments, and

A NIGHT IN THE WOODS.

I proposed that we camp where we were till morning. There was plenty of dry wood in the vicinity, and by cutting a few boughs we could have fixed up a camp beside the pier, where we could have passed the night quite comfortably. But Jack did not take kindly to my proposition, saying we could reach Upton by ten o'clock, and have a comfortable bed to sleep in, which would be much better than camping out. For my own part, however, I was disposed to let well enough alone; for neither of us had ever been over the road, and only knew about it from the Upton guides, who occasionally traveled it. Very foolishly I allowed myself to be persuaded against my better judgment, and leaving the river we plunged into the woods.

We found the road to be worse than our most vivid fancy had painted. It was so indistinct that it would have been a hard job to have followed it in the middle of the day, and now it was so dark that one could scarcely discern objects three feet away. To add to our discomfort the road was badly grown up, and it was actually easier to get along just outside of where the road had been than try to follow the old track. Windfalls were also numerous, and retarded our progress, and in turning aside to avoid these we frequently lost all traces of the road, and would have to hunt some time before we found it again.

Tired and panting we struggled on, and at eight o'clock we had not made more than a mile, and further locomotion, except by groping our way, was impossible, it had become so dark.

"Ready to camp yet, Jack?" I asked, as we stopped a moment to rest.

"No, sir; I am going to get to Upton to-night."

"Well, my boy, your pluck is good; but, mark my words, "you won't sleep in a hotel to-night."

"I'll make a try for it, any way," he said, as he started forward once more.

For the next three hours we stumbled and scrambled along; now falling flat over the decaying trunk of some tree that lay across our path, then bumping our noses against standing trees, obtaining the first intimation of their proximity in this manner.

To vary the fun we occasionally barked our shins over huge boulders, that we could feel but not see. The night was intensely dark, — so dark you could almost feel it, — and not a star to be seen. Indeed, as we were in a thick growth, you could not see the sky half the time when you looked up.

Struggling on with more courage than common-sense we at last reached a swamp, and stopped and lit a match, and then a piece of paper, to make out where we were. By the light of the burning paper Jack looked at his watch and found it was eleven o'clock. Just beyond us, to the left, we saw a little knoll that looked comparatively dry, and we made our way to it. As we reached the middle of it Jack dropped his gun and overcoat, and exclaimed : —

THE LAST MATCH.

A NIGHT IN THE WOODS.   63

"It is no use, Captain, I give it up!"

"Then the sooner we make a fire the better," I replied, with a quiet smile at his discomfiture.

Lighting a match and another piece of paper we began searching for a dry stump or a white birch tree, but, to our disgust, could find neither.

We appeared to be surrounded on all sides by a thick growth of firs, the only other trees I saw being two yellow birches, one about three, and the other about eight, inches in diameter.

Feeling my way to the larger one, for my paper had now burned out, I succeeded by the aid of my knife in getting about two handfuls of yellow birch-bark, — poor stuff for kindling a fire.

I put this in my hat, and feeling about under the tree found a few dry leaves; these I added to the bark, then made my way back to Jack, who had managed in spite of the darkness to get three or four rocks together to build our fire on.

I emptied my hat of the bark and leaves, then went through my pockets and produced all the paper I could find about my clothing, while Jack gathered a few dead limbs from a fir near us.

By this time it had grown very cold, and both of us were shivering with the chill night air, and we really needed a fire as much for its warmth as for the light it would furnish.

Fumbling in my vest-pocket with my cold fingers, I was vexed to find that I had only three matches left, and I knew that Jack had used all of his some time before. I scratched the first match; it sputtered a little, then went out. The second one burned some better, but went out before I could light the bark. Things were getting desperate. Only one match and a cold night before us.

"Only one match left, Jack," I said, as I threw the second one away.

"What!" and there was a world of meaning in that little word as he pronounced it.

"Just as I tell you. Now hold your hat near me. If this match goes back on us we shall have to dance to keep warm."

Jack held his hat in such a position that when I ignited the match he sheltered the blaze from the wind, and working carefully I succeeded in catching fire to the paper and the light bark of the yellow birch. For fear it would be blown out, for the wind had come up quite strong in the last hour, we held our hats to windward of the flame until it had grown a little, and then pushed the dry twigs from the fir over it.

While I attended to the fire Jack broke off some more of the dead limbs from the fir, then taking the axe managed to hack down the smallest of the yellow birches, and cut it into lengths about two feet long. Piling on a good half of this fuel, we soon had a fair fire blazing, and while Jack took a rest, for it was warm work chopping with our sharp(?) axe, I cut down a couple of good-sized firs, trimming the limbs all off,

A NIGHT IN THE WOODS.

and divided them into two piles. Those that were dead or dry I threw toward the fire, and the live or green ones I threw into a separate pile, to be used in building a brush camp.

After that I cut up the trunks of the firs into firewood, and then tackled the large yellow birch, hacking about half-way through it.

By this time I was willing to turn the axe over to my companion in misery, and while he finished felling the birch I selected a place for our camp, and broke off some more fir boughs to use in its construction.

After the birch fell Jack hacked off a lot of the smaller limbs, and we piled them on the fire until we had a glorious blaze, throwing a circle of light several rods from us. This enabled us to take a good look about us, and we found we were but a few steps from the road, on a slight elevation of ground, a round knoll, which sloped off on all sides to a swamp.

But although we strained our eyes to catch a glimpse of some white birches, or even another yellow birch, they were not to be seen, the entire forest as far as our light extended showing only firs, with a very few cedars.

While Jack took care of the fire I went for some small firs, and cut down about fifteen of them, then dragged them up to the fire, and trimmed off all the boughs, and threw them on the pile with the others; then I cut the poles of an even length, about eight feet, and sharpened five of them at one end.

We were now ready to set up our camp, but before commencing we cut up the balance of our yellow birch into small pieces and threw some of them on the fire.

Selecting the five poles I had sharpened at the end, we drove four of them into the ground, each two crossed near the top, and about eight feet of space between them. The fifth stake we drove down perpendicularly at the back of the camp, the bottom being in the middle of the two crossed stakes at that end. Then we took one of the other poles, and laid it into the crotches formed by the four end poles, and that made our ridge-pole.

We now had a skeleton frame, tent-shaped. To enable us to cover it more easily we took six of the other poles, and sharpening the larger ends set them into the ground a little, on a line with the others, and rested the tops against the ridge-pole. Then we began to wattle on our fir boughs, and soon had both sides covered. At the back end we stood up several small thick firs, that effectually closed that part. The front of our camp we left open, so as to obtain the heat from the fire, which was about six feet from us.

When this was done we threw fresh fuel on the fire, and by the additional light went and stripped all the cedar trees we could find of their limbs, and brought them to the camp and spread them on the ground to lie on.

"Any pitch on your hands, Captain?" asked Jack, as we rested a moment from our labor.

"Only about half an inch thick. I think fir is the meanest wood that grows."

"Poor stuff for firewood, any way, and the pitch is making my hands sore; but before we lay down we shall have to cut two or three of those large firs, for the birch won't last us till morning."

It was now one o'clock, and thinking that if we intended to get any sleep at all, the sooner the wood was cut the better, we went at it.

Relieving each other at short intervals we worked steadily for about an hour, and procured quite a pile of wood, such as it was. After throwing a lot of it on the fire we spread Jack's coat over the cedar boughs, and used mine, which was the heaviest, to cover us with. We lay pretty snugly, the better to keep warm, and the dog crawled up to us, and stretched out by my side. It was now two o'clock, and a few stray snow-flakes were finding their way to the ground; but, overcome with fatigue, and unmindful of the weather, we dropped to sleep at once.

In about an hour I awoke feeling chilly, and I turned out and piled the remainder of the wood on the fire, calculating that it would last until daylight, which would be between four and five o'clock. I found an inch of snow had fallen, and that it was snowing very fast.

As I crawled back to our primitive couch Jack awoke and wanted to know what the matter was. I told him I had been replenishing the fire, and that there was an inch of snow on the ground.

"I don't care if there's a foot," he replied, drowsily, and turned over and went to sleep.

We slept without waking again until about half-past four, when Jack roused up and awoke me. I felt stiff and cold, and every bone in my body seemed to ache. I was not at all sorry to get up.

"Come, Captain, let's leave this God-forsaken hole. Daylight is just breaking, and we can follow the road all right now. I think I took cold last night; I feel as if I had been pounded from head to foot."

We picked up our things, scattered the fire, for it had stopped snowing, and after I had written on a card "Camp Misery," and the date, and pinned it to a tree, we headed for Upton.

About two inches of snow had fallen, loading the trees and bushes, and we found it very disagreeable traveling. We took it easy, however, and reached the hotel about eight o'clock.

CHAPTER IV.

*"And seated round the blazing hearth,
In song and jest the time was spent."*

KILLING TIME.

THE sight of that house afforded us unspeakable pleasure. Hungry and footsore we took refuge in the office, where we found a half-dozen sportsmen and guides, who stared at us with open-mouthed wonder. We dropped our things, pulled off our overcoats, and had a wash, which, after the way we had passed the night, was most refreshing.

Mr. Godwin, the landlord, soon came in, and his eyes opened when he saw us. I have no doubt we looked like a couple of tramps.

"Where did you drop down from, Captain, at this time in the morning? I supposed you were at the Upper Dam."

"We left there yesterday morning, and, on account of several little drawbacks, we had to stop in the woods last night. But I wish you would start some breakfast for us; we have not had anything of any consequence to eat since yesterday morning."

"You don't say so; well, I should think you would be hungry;" and he went off to order our breakfast.

When he returned I gave him the particulars of our tramp, and he told us that they had taken all the boats off the river the day they broke camp at the Middle Dam.

"If I had known you were coming out this way I should have left a boat for you. You are going over to Andover, I suppose."

"Not now. We have started for Parmachenee. Did the 'Diamond' go up the Magalloway this morning?"

"Yes, and she won't make another trip until Friday; so you can stop two or three days with me."

"I don't know about that. We ought to take a row-boat and push on. But I will decide after breakfast."

That welcome meal was soon announced, and to say that Jack and I did not do it justice would be doing us an injustice. Hot biscuit, beefsteak, eggs, coffee, and griddle-cakes disappeared with such celerity that the girl who waited upon us began to turn pale, fancying, I suppose, that we should eat her if the food gave out.

However all things must come to an end sometime, and so did that delicious and ever-memorable breakfast, after which we adjourned to the office, and had a smoke.

There were two or three guests at the hotel, who were staying there for a few days' shooting, and one of them, a doctor from Brooklyn, New York, with whom

I was acquainted, urged me strongly to stop until Friday, and then go as far as we could on the steamer.

"It's a cold, raw day," said he, "and you will find it rough and disagreeable on the lake in a small boat. You will find it more to your taste to sit around this fire than to pull a boat twenty-five or thirty miles in the wind. See how pleasant the fire looks! Just keep quiet, and I'll tell a story, and you shall sing a song."

"I don't doubt your ability for telling the story, but would much prefer some one besides myself to sing the song."

"Then we'll have the colonel sing the song," and the doctor looked at his military friend and smiled.

"You never heard me sing, Doctor, or you would not have made that remark."

The doctor laughed and winked at me, and then said : —

"Just rest here contented, and to-morrow we will go out after partridges."

Jack had gone out-doors, and I hunted him up and asked him what he thought about stopping until Friday where we were, and he said he was willing if I was.

I told him the doctor had said that partridges were plenty, and the next day we would go out for some.

Accordingly we stopped at the hotel until Friday morning. The weather was disagreeable most of the time, being very cold and windy, with frequent snow-squalls.

After it was decided that we would wait to go on Friday's boat we took the axe that had caused us so much hard work, and ground it until it had a decent edge on it once more. Jack declared, as he ran his finger along the edge, that it would cut a hair. I laughed at his remark, and told him that perhaps it would if he laid the hair on a block.

We were promptly "on deck" when the dinner-bell rang, and as we walked into the dining-room the pretty table-girl looked surprised, evidently thinking that we had eaten breakfast enough to last all day. Her looks did not trouble us, however, and we found the dinner as much to our liking as the breakfast had been. As we arose from the table the girl asked Jack if we were going to stop at the house a great while. He told her, "Only a few days." She looked relieved at his answer, and informed him that, if we thought of stopping a great while, Godwin would have to hire another table-girl, for it took all her time to wait on us. We laughed; but I thought her remarks a trifle impertinent, as we had only met her for the first time at the breakfast-table, and as Jack did not seem to have a reply ready I determined to get even with her.

She was quite tall, but rather thin, although her features were remarkably pretty, and a thought struck me.

"Did you know," I asked her, assuming a serious face, "that Mr. Godwin is not going to have you any longer?"

DUCK-SHOOTING ON UMBAGOG LAKE.

"Why not?" she asked, a shadow of alarm flitting across her face.

"Because you are long enough already," I returned, with a triumphant laugh, in which Jack joined, and we left the room on the jump.

Although it was a rough day we did not feel like stopping in the house all the time, and soon after dinner walked down to the river-bank, launched a row-boat, and pulled down to the lake, a distance of two miles, owing to the crooks in the river, while in an air-line it was not more than half as far.

Near B Point we fell in with some black ducks, and after chasing them some distance around the shore Jack obtained a good shot at them, just after they had left the water, and brought down three. These we secured, but the remainder of the flock flew to such a distance that we did not think it worth while to follow them, but pulled back to the house. The ducks I took to the kitchen, and asked the cook to serve them for breakfast the next morning.

We passed the evening in the office listening to fishing stories from those present, who seemed to vie with each other in telling the most monstrous yarns. I never saw a fisherman yet who liked to be outdone by his comrades in telling about his exploits in the fishing-line; but, although it is a scaly business, a fisherman was never known to lie.

We went out Wednesday morning after partridges, leaving the house at half-past eight. We carried a lunch with us, and made a day of it. We first followed an old woods road back of the house nearly to the lake, picking up five birds on the way. From the "Heywood Clearing" we struck through the woods to the "Tyler Place," and then worked that vicinity thoroughly for two hours. By this time it was one o'clock, and we were hungry.

The doctor called a rest; and, sitting on a fallen tree, we sampled our luncheons, and quaffed our thirst from a spring a few feet away. The cold, sparkling spring-water was good enough for me; but, by the doctor's advice, the others had a "stick" in their water, to keep it from hurting them. Said stick was produced by the doctor, and appeared in the shape of a wicker-bound flask, which was passed around, each taking his turn. Then we had a smoke, and after that made our way back by a logging road, that ended near the hotel.

Although the weather had been against us, the day being very cold, and cloudy most of the time, we had met with excellent luck, and four of us succeeded in bagging seventeen birds, and that night at supper we tried their quality.

Thursday morning, after breakfast, we walked to the stores, two miles away, and purchased a few things that we thought would be necessary for the Parmachenee trip, but which we should have done without had it not been for our unexpected wait.

Jack, who was developing an interest in the table-girl, invested in peanuts and candy for her benefit, and made the presentation at dinner-time, loitering for that purpose until all had left the room but Clara and himself.

In the afternoon I went off down on the meadow below the house with Mr. Godwin, to inspect some traps he had set there, and we found three muskrats and one otter in them. The otter was the largest I had ever seen, and very handsome. When we returned to the house we found Morse and Sargeant there, two professional hunters who lived in the neighborhood, and they said the skin was worth from eight to twelve dollars. But fur was higher then than now.

"Killed any bears lately, Luman?" inquired Jack of one of the guides, winking at me, as he asked the question, to attract my attention.

"Yes, yes," returned the guide, earnestly; "found one in my trap, over near C Pond, yesterday."

"Was he dead?" I inquired.

"No, no, not when I found him. But I put a couple of bullets into him that settled his hash."

"How much did he weigh?" queried Jack.

"Between three and four hundred, and he was as fat as a hog."

"That is a 'weigh' they have," laughed Jack. But Luman did not see the point of the joke. In fact, he didn't "catch on."

"Are there many bears about this fall?" I asked, hoping to start the old fellow on a bear story.

"Gorry, yes. Plenty of them. They've been killing sheep in Grafton all the fall."

"I should think the people would turn out and hunt them," said one of the gentlemen present.

"Wall, they had orter," answered the hunter, who somehow did not seem inclined to talk much, and soon after he and his companion left the house.

In the evening I wrote some letters home, as it was the best chance I should have for some time, while Jack played cards with the three guests, and, much to his chagrin, himself and his partner were badly beaten, the game being whist.

Through the Ice.

CHAPTER V.

*"A fresher gale
Begins to wave the wood and stir the lake."*—THOMSON.

A SAIL ON THE "DIAMOND."

FRIDAY morning we went down to the steamer, and found the river was frozen over as far as we could see, the ice being about one-fourth of an inch thick. The sun was shining, but there were a large number of clouds in the sky, and it looked more like a storm than pleasant weather.

"We're all ridy to start, Captain," said Chris to me, as we walked on board, and the engineer began working the engine back and forth to break up the ice around us.

A few revolutions of the wheels accomplished this, and, hauling in the lines, the captain rang to "go ahead," and in a minute later we were ploughing our way down the river, the boat scattering the ice in all directions. As we neared the mouth of the river we came to open water, and upon entering the lake found it clear of ice, except in a few small coves.

It was a very sharp morning, the wind coming out quite strong, and we found it so cold on deck that we were glad to take shelter in the engine-room, while the old steamer puffed her way onward.

"Take a seat by the biler, Cap'n," called Chris, as we entered. "I thought ye would foind it too cold outside, while we are crossin' the lake. It won't be so bad when we get into the river. And so ye are goin' up to Parmachenee? Faith, I'd like to be goin' along wid ye."

"I wish you were," said Jack. "We shall probably have a good time."

"Were you ever up there?" I asked.

"No, but I've bin over on the Diamond, and I always wanted to go to Parmachenee. I couldn't go in better company, byes, and if I could lave the boat I'd go in a minute. But yees see Jim couldn't get back wid the steamer."

"I should say not," replied Jack.

"Is there much large game around Parmachenee?" I inquired.

"I've heard fellers say there was who lumbered up there. One of the river-drivers told me this spring that he shot a moose up there last winter, and he said caribou were plenty as foxes."

"How plenty were the foxes?" asked Jack, with a wink at me.

"I didn't ax him," replied the engineer, with a grin; "but I will the next toime I see him."

"We are nearly to the outlet, aren't we, Chris?" inquired Jack, who had walked over to the port side of the steamer, and was looking out of the window.

Chris glanced outside and then replied: —

"Yes, we're off against Moll's Rock now; that's it, that rocky p'int ye see, and we'll be out of the lake in a few minutes."

"Why do they call it Moll's Rock?" queried Jack, who was one of the most inquisitive fellows I ever met.

"Because an old Injun woman used to live there, and her name was Molly Molasses. She was Metalluc's squaw."

"She had a sweet name," said Jack, laughing.

"Probably the latter part of her name was suggested by her color, rather than her disposition," I added, laughing in sympathy.

"Ye may laugh all ye please, byes, but she certainly lived there, and whin she wint up Magalloway she used to carry her canoe across that narrow strip of land there;" and Chris pointed to the place.

Jack and I took a look in the direction indicated, and I wondered how many times Molly had ever crossed there.

"It is called 'Moll's Carry,'" added the engineer, "and ye'll get a good look at it as we go down river. We've rin across that carry wid this boat at high water."

After entering the Androscoggin River Jack and I went out on deck again to watch for ducks. We saw quite a number; also two blue herons, and a magnificent bald eagle, but did not get near enough to shoot any of them.

Chris came out in time to see the eagle, and, with a twinkle in his eye, remarked, "Thim aigles can be caught, Cap'n, if ye get near enough to put salt on their tails."

"Oh, get out!" replied Jack, laughing; "that tale is too old. Give us something new."

"How much time shall we have at Errol, Chris?"

"Fifteen or twenty minutes, perhaps more, Cap'n. But if ye go ashore I'll whistle whin we're ridy to leave."

"That's right," replied Jack. "Give us time to look around a little. I never was in Errol before."

"Faith, and ye haven't missed much; the house and the dam is all there is for ye to see. But ye oughter be here in the spring once, if ye wanter see miskeetors and black flies. Errol bates all the places in the wurld for them. We don't make very long stops here in the spring whin we land, I tell ye."

"Are the mosquitoes as large as they are in New Jersey?"

"I don't know about that, Captain. But many of thim here will weigh a pound."

"Out in New Jersey they have to house their cattle every night during mosquito time to keep the mosquitoes from carrying them off."

Chris looked at me square in the eye for a second,

and then walked away. He was silenced for the time being.

After passing the mouth of the Magalloway we found a little ice in the river; but the steamer made her way through it easily, and we reached Errol Dam all right at half-past ten.

While the captain and engineer of the steamer were unloading some freight Jack and I took a run on shore, and Spot scared up a partridge which Jack shot. We thought there might be more in the vicinity, and were encouraging the dog to find them, when we heard the hoarse whistle of the steamer, and knew that our time was up.

We hurried down to the boat, and found the fasts all cast off, and that they were only waiting for us. We jumped on board, and the steamer started to retrace her course, the Magalloway, up which river we were bound, emptying into the Androscoggin four miles above Errol Dam.

" Ha! ha! byes, ye came near gettin' left that toime," said the good-natured Hibernian who had charge of the engine.

" Why, Chris, you don't mean to say you were going to run away from us?"

" Faith, I warnt, Captain, but I whistled so as to hurry yees a little. Got a shot at a partridge, didn't ye?"

" Yes, Jack shot it, and I shall have it for dinner."

" Will you?" inquired Jack. " Where do I come in?"

"Oh, you can come in at the door, or the window, just as you please! But if you shoot the partridge, and I eat it, I am sure that is a fair division of labor."

"Yes, altogether too fair. You remind me of the Irishman who had quarreled with his wife, and proposed to her that they divide the house even, and told her 'he'd be after kaping the inside, and she could have the outside.'"

"And that did not suit her, I suppose," I replied, with a laugh. "Women are so unreasonable."

"There comes a blue heron," cried Jack, pointing to the bird, and with careful aim he fired, the only result being to make the heron swerve in his flight.

"Wait till we get into the Magalloway, and ye'll get a shot at some ducks. We see lots of 'em every day we go up there."

Half an hour after leaving the dam the boat made a sharp turn to the left and entered the Magalloway. From its mouth to the landing was eight miles by the river but not more than half that in a straight line.

The river is one of the most beautiful in the world. Narrow and crooked, it twists and turns to all points of the compass. The banks are from three to six feet high, and are thickly wooded on both sides. In some places the large elms whose branches spread out over the river nearly meet in an arch overhead, and the forest is reflected from the quiet water as plainly as from a mirror. Among the growth are many tall firs, hoary with age, and draped and festooned with long, trailing, light-colored moss, that gives them a charming and fantastic appearance, reminding one of Longfellow's lines : —

"This is the forest primeval. The murmuring pines and the hemlocks,
Bearded with moss, and in garments green, indistinct in the twilight,
Stand like Druids of old, with voices sad and prophetic,
Stand like harpers hoar, with beards that rest on their bosoms."

There are quite a number of small ponds and "logons" a short distance back from the river, scattered along for many miles. This is true of both the Lower and Upper Magalloway. These little bodies of water are excellent feeding-places for wild fowl and deer, as their borders, and sometimes their entire surface, are covered with a peculiar kind of grass, also water lilies and other aquatic plants.

On deck, near the bow, Jack and I took our station, and were soon joined by the engineer.

Soon after turning a sharp bend of the river the steamer passed Pulpit Rock, and Chris pointed it out to them, saying it was a favorite spot for camping out.

A few rods beyond, the engineer discovered a fox trotting along the starboard side of the river, and called our attention to the animal.

"We will have a shot at it," I exclaimed, and we watched Reynard anxiously; he stopped occasionally to investigate, and Chris said he was after mussels or musk-rats, he did not know which.

Captain Tenny had now sighted the fox, and he slanted the steamer toward him.

"There's a chance for you, Jack," he called out from the wheel-house. "See if you can't get that fox. His skin is worth a dollar and a half."

"I'll warm him, if we get near enough," answered Jack, softly.

A moment or two more and the steamer was within gunshot; but, just as we fired, Reynard turned and saw us, and made tracks for the woods. He was out of sight in a moment, and we never knew whether he was struck or not.

"Better luck next time," cried the captain, as he closed the window, for it was colder in the wheel-house than it was down on deck.

"I am sorry we did not get that fox," said Jack, as he put fresh charges in his gun.

"We may see another before we git to the landin'," the engineer replied. "Some days we see two or three of them on this trip."

Shortly after this the steamer came in sight of a large brook on the left-hand side of the river. Chris told us it was Bear Brook; but nary a "b'ar" did we see.

A few moments more brought us up to Bottle Brook, also on the left side of the river, and here we saw the first signs of civilization we had met with since leaving Errol, in the shape of a small log-cabin.

The engineer, who seemed to be an encyclopædia of

the country, told us that an Indian squaw resided there, and that she had a white husband.

"I don't admire his taste," declared Jack, contemptuously.

Two men now made their appearance from the cabin, and, taking fishing-poles that stood against one end of it, went down to the brook. They waved their hats as the steamer swept by.

"Why do they call that stream Bottle Brook, Chris?"

"Faix, Cap'n, ye have me there, for I don't know. It's been called Bottle Brook iver since I came into this country; but I guess"—and he smiled—"it is because there are so many bottles opened there by fishermen."

"I suppose the first fellow who opened a bottle there threw it into the stream and christened the brook," added Jack.

"In a horn he did," I remarked.

"You mean he took a horn when he did," laughed my companion.

Just beyond Bottle Brook the boat swept around a sharp turn, and Chris told Jack to be ready. As we turned the point we saw seven black ducks, and, as they rose, Jack blazed away at them, and I gave them three shots from my revolver. Three of them were knocked over, and it has always been an open question between Jack and I as to who killed the ducks. But of course I know.

Chris stopped the steamer, and he and Jack went out in the small boat and picked them up. On their return we steamed up river again. Although we saw several flocks afterwards we did not get near enough to any of them to shoot successfully.

We passed another house, which Chris said was Chase's, and then turned around a long point, known as "Sharp Shins." It was the sharpest turn we had made on the river, and I thought the boat would not make it; but the captain brought her around after a while, but he had a narrow escape from running aground.

A little after twelve we arrived at Littlehale's landing in Wentworth's Location, and were met by a team, which took us all up to the Brown Farm, a mile and three-quarters distant, where we took dinner at the Berlin Mills House. We had our ducks and partridge cooked, and found them decidedly toothsome.

Chris and Captain Tenny did not have much time to spare, as they wished to get home before dark, and they started to walk back immediately after dinner, the team not going down.

We bade them "good-by" and shook hands with them before they left, and told them we hoped to meet them again, and have another ride on the steamer.

They reciprocated our sentiments, and wished us good luck, and then left at a rapid gait, for they were already behind time.

A Lucky Shot.

CHAPTER VI.

"The stately stag, that seems so stout,
  By yelping hounds at day is set;
The swiftest bird, that flies about,
  Is caught at length in fowler's net;
The greatest fish, in deepest brook,
  Is soon deceived by subtle hook."

A SUCCESSFUL HUNT.

PETE BARLEYCORN, who had charge of the hotel, introduced us after dinner to the agent of the Berlin Mills Company, and from him we learned that the steamer would only make two more trips up the river that season, on the following Tuesday and Friday. I told him we were going up to Parmachenee, and that the length of our stay would depend entirely on the weather. I asked him about a team to take us to the Upper Magalloway settlement, six miles above, and found we could procure one at the house.

He said partridges were thick in the vicinity, and that we could have some good sport there that afternoon if we would stop a few hours. He directed us to a piece of hard-wood growth that began on a hill at the back of the house and ran down to Sturtevant's Pond.

As we had not intended going beyond the Upper Settlement that day a delay of a few hours did not matter much, and a partridge hunt seemed to offer an advantageous manner of passing away the time. Besides, there was a possibility of meeting with larger game, as the country back of the Brown Farm was a wilderness for miles.

Chris had told us, while coming up on the steamer, of several deer being shot in the vicinity of Sturtevant's Pond in the last two years, and it might be our good fortune to see one, even if we did not shoot it. I concluded, therefore, to visit the pond and see what luck Dame Fortune had in store for us.

Calling the dog, Jack and I started off for the woods, and, reaching the forest, beat our way carefully through it, until we stood on the shore of the pond. Here we found signs of deer, and a moment later were startled by a noise to the left, and, looking in that direction, saw a deer swimming across the pond.

Although Jack had nothing but bird-shot in his gun he took careful aim at the deer and fired, while I blazed away until my revolver was empty.

"If we only had a boat now we could overtake him," cried Jack, in a wild state of excitement.

I run my eye along the shore in each direction, but nothing in the shape of a boat was to be seen. Taking out a box of cartridges I reloaded my revolver, and then proposed to Jack that we should make our way around the shore of the pond, in hopes to get another shot at the deer. Although my proposition was doubtful, Jack accepted it, and we pushed our way along as fast as possible, taking a glance at the deer occasionally to see how fast he was getting along.

We soon found, however, that we stood no sight for getting another shot at him, for, before we were half-way around to the point for which he was heading, he had reached the shore and disappeared in the woods. As we knew it would be useless to follow him then we turned toward the house.

"Confound the luck!" cried Jack, in no very good humor; "we have lost that deer just because there was no boat here. I should think Brown would keep one in the pond."

"Don't cry for spilled milk," I returned cheerfully; "if we have lost the deer that need not prevent our losing the partridges. Find them, Spot!" I cried, and the dog wagged his tail and started ahead. His short, sharp bark soon announced that he had treed something, and upon reaching him we found seven partridges on a young spruce, and killed five of them.

Picking up our game we moved on. All through the vicinity the cover for partridges was excellent, there being a plentiful sprinkling of young spruces among the hard wood.

Suddenly Jack stopped and examined the ground in an excited manner. I was a few feet behind him, and hurried up to see what had attracted his attention.

"Look here," cried Jack, who was down on his knees, as I stood beside him; "do you see that?" pointing to a track in the earth.

"Yes," I replied; "what of it?"

"It's a bear-track."

I looked at it with more interest.

"Are you sure of it?" I inquired.

"Of course I am. Don't you think I know a bear-track when I see one?"

"That's a debatable question," I returned; "but we'll mention it to Pete, so that he can look after his sheep to-night."

"Suppose we try and follow him," suggested Jack.

"Not much," I answered. "I think we shall be more successful hunting partridges than we shall trailing a bear that may be ten miles away from here now."

"I would like to kill one mighty well," asserted Jack.

"So would I; but we need rifles if we are going bear-hunting. I don't care to meet one while I have only this little revolver to defend myself with. Let's move along; we have no time to spare;" and I started homewards.

Just before getting out of the woods we run upon another flock of seven birds, out of which we shot four. We tried to find the other three, but did not succeed, and as it was four o'clock we gave up all idea of any more shooting, and again started for the hotel, which we reached after an absence of about four hours. As soon as we arrived at the house one of the men harnessed a horse to a single buckboard, and we started off, having given five of our birds to the hotel people.

Our ride up the valley would have been enjoyable had it not been so cold, and verging on darkness. We obtained a good idea of the country, however, and the driver pointed out in succession Mount Dustan, the Diamond Peaks, and Half-Moon Mountain, — all of them standing on the opposite side of the road and the river.

The swift Diamond empties into the Magalloway, about a mile from the hotel, its waters rushing down between Mount Dustan and the Diamond Peaks. It drains a large extent of country, and is the outlet of the Diamond Ponds.

The driver told us we would find good sport if we went up on the Dead Diamond, a branch of the Swift, and informed us that large game was very plenty up there.

".I will take a look at that country some other time," I replied. "I am not going to Parmachenee Lake especially for hunting, but more to see the country."

"We might go over on the Diamond next fall," suggested Jack.

"Yes, we might. But next fall is too far ahead. We may all be dead before that time."

The driver now called our attention to a rough-looking log-house, on the side of which was stretched a bearskin, and told us that a great bear-hunter lived there, and added that this was the third skin the man had taken that fall.

"Does he shoot them?" inquired Jack.

"No, he traps them. He caught the bear that hide came off from up to the head of the falls."

"Do you mean Aziscohos Falls?" I asked.

"Yes. Bears are awful thick around there and on the mountain."

"We shall have to keep our eyes open, when we go up there," remarked Jack.

"You needn't be afeered; the bears won't trouble you as long as you let 'em alone. I have met three in the woods at different times, and never had one show fight yet. They allers run as soon as they see ye, or wind ye. Come, git up, er lang!" and he brought the whip down on the horse's rump.

Three of us were rather too much load for the horse, or else he was lazy; and we were crowded in the most uncomfortable manner on the seat. It was tiresome riding, especially so after it became dark, with the landscape blotted out.

"I am getting about enough of this," declared Jack, as the buckboard went over a rough place in the road, shaking us up, and nearly throwing us out. "I guess I'll walk the rest of the way."

"I wouldn't," said the driver; "we are most there, and it is so dark you'll find it bad footing."

A drive of a little more than an hour brought us to

A Backwoods Residence.

the Upper Settlement, and as there was no hotel here we had to skirmish around a little to find a place to stop in. It really seemed like being out of the world, to find a village without a public house.

After trying two or three houses we went to a Mr. Fickett's, and he agreed to give us supper, lodging, and breakfast, if Jack and I would occupy the same bed and room. He had some men stopping with him that night who were thrashing grain in the vicinity, and that made the house crowded. As it was "Hobson's choice," that or nothing, we agreed, and the fellow who had brought us up river left our things and drove back. We were ushered into the kitchen, a fair-sized room, with a large brick fireplace, in which a cheerful fire blazed, and we had become so chilled during our ride that we were glad to avail ourselves of its genial warmth. The table was in the middle of the floor when we went in, and, by the time we had become comfortably warm, supper was ready, and we were hungry enough to do it justice.

After supper I asked Mrs. Fickett if she would cook our partridges for breakfast, and she promised to. Then we drew up to the fire and smoked, and listened to bear stories.

From the talk of the men it appeared that bears were very thick there that fall, and had killed quite a number of sheep in the settlement.

"These fellows can tell bare lies as well as bear .

stories," whispered Jack to me with a smile, during a lull in the conversation.

"Yes, that little fellow, smoking the short-stemmed pipe, is very proficient at drawing the long bow. He would make a good soap manufacturer."

"Why so?"

"Because there is so much lie in him. But I have heard enough of it," and I arose to my feet.

Feeling quite tired after our day's racket we went to bed early, and obtained a good night's rest.

CHAPTER VII.

"Out of the bosom of the air,
 Out of the cloud-folds of her garments shaken,
Over the woodlands brown and bare,
Over the harvest-fields forsaken,
 Silent, and soft, and slow
 Descends the snow."—LONGFELLOW.

UP THE RIVER.

I WAS the first to awaken in the morning, and, jumping out of bed, I pulled up the curtain to get a look out-doors, and to my surprise found the ground covered with snow, and the air filled with the fast-falling flakes.

"How is the weather out?" asked Jack, who had been awakened by my noise.

"Bad. It is snowing as hard as I ever saw it, and there are already about three inches on the ground."

"I suppose you'll give up going, then."

"Not much. It will take more than a little snow to frighten me."

"But it will be no fool of a joke to get snowed up in the woods."

"I don't intend to get snowed up; but I started for Parmachenee Lake, and, by the 'great horn spoon,' I am going there before I return home, if I go alone."

"If you go, Captain, I shall. But it will be anything but a pleasant trip."

"Can't help it; we must take the weather as it comes, and do the best we can;" and I finished dressing and went out to the kitchen.

Jack soon joined me, and again attempted to persuade me to give up the trip. But, although he was heartily seconded by Mr. Fickett, who thought there would be a heavy storm, I would not give up the idea.

Having lived nearly all my life in Boston and New York, it did not seem possible to me that we could have much of a snow-storm the second week in October. I did not know the ways of the weather clerk in that Northern climate then as well as I do now, or I should have had no doubts on the subject at all.

I have heard some of the people who live along the Magalloway river, in speaking of the weather, say that "they had nine months winter and three months late in the fall." And, although that statement is something of an exaggeration, it is a pretty fair average description of the weather.

As I had been hard at work all summer, looking forward to this trip with a great deal of pleasure, I hated to give it up, and determined to push on until I reached the lake, regardless of consequences.

As it turned out I had more pleasure in the antici-

CROSSING THE CARRY.

pation than the realization of my wish; but, then, that is the way with many others in this world. We chase phantoms from childhood to the grave, and never catch them on this side of the Styx. Perhaps in the unknown world toward which we are all drifting we shall be more fortunate.

We had a splendid breakfast, our partridges being nicely cooked, and those, with excellent coffee, good biscuit, and baked potatoes, made a meal fit for a king.

After breakfast I had Mrs. Fickett put us up a large firkin of cooked food, as we would have no chance to get anything more to eat until we reached Sunday Pond Camp, and we did not expect to get there until late at night.

At eight o'clock we left the house, and tramped up the road a short distance, then turned off into a pasture, and, striking the road that led to the head of Aziscohos Falls, trudged steadily onward. It was three miles to the head of the Falls, and the walking was horrible, — snow, slush, and mud, and the damp snow wet our clothing as quickly as if it had been rain. However we made the best of it, and laughed and joked as we plodded our way along.

We called the firkin our commissary department, and, as it was rather heavy to "sack," took turns in carrying it.

"By Jove! Captain, we ought to have tried to hire Fickett to carry us to the head of the Falls with his team. This is the worst walking I ever experienced."

"It is nothing after you get used to it. It will give you a good appetite for dinner, Jack."

Just then Jack slipped, and came down in the slush; as he rose to his feet he let off a string of verbal fireworks that would have made a missionary turn pale, and to save my life I could not help laughing.

He glared at me a moment as if he would like to eat me, and then renewed his struggle with the elements.

"Come, old fellow," I said, when I thought he had recovered his temper a little, "carry the firkin awhile, for I am tired."

He took it willingly, and we jogged along in silence for a spell, ruminating over the delightful (?) time we were having. After making another laborious half mile, Jack broke out with:—

"It seems to me, Captain, that this grub is confounded heavy."

"I hope not," I replied, laughing; "at least I hope the bread is light."

The words had scarcely left my mouth when I caught my toe under a root, and down I went into the mud and snow. I felt less like joking than I had a minute before.

"How do you like it?" queried Jack, laughing, as I scrambled to my feet, feeling, and no doubt looking, disgusted.

"Don't like it a bit," I replied, savagely, as I brushed the slush from my clothing. "How far do you suppose we have come?"

"I don't believe we are more than half-way over, Captain, and I shall be almighty glad when we get there. I had rather row a boat in this storm all day than travel over such an infernal road. I don't believe the people ever work on it."

"Well, it is time they did, but I suppose it is not a county road."

The dog was having about as hard a time as we were, for in some places the mud was so soft, and with the snow so deep, that he could scarcely wallow through it, and he stopped frequently to rest.

By this time the trees were getting badly loaded with the fast-falling flakes, and, as we occasionally brushed by them, we found this another disagreeable feature. Several times a lot of snow went into my neck, and before I could get it off it would melt, and run down my back, adding to my discomfort.

Once a large fir limb, completely loaded with snow, struck Jack fair in the face, and brushed off his cap. This was followed by another exhibition of verbal fireworks. I suppose I did wrong to laugh at such times, but I could not help it.

To make amends I relieved him of the " commissary department," and that had a soothing effect.

Just as we began to wonder if we had not lost our way we heard the roaring of water, and concluded that we could not be a great way from the river.

We reached the landing at the head of the Falls at half-past nine, and found more snow there than we had seen before. It was quite evident that the storm was coming from the direction in which we were going.

It was a wild-looking place where the carry road ended, just beyond the commencement of the swift water; straggling trees of various kinds overhung the dark current below us. The river falls about two hundred feet in a distance of two miles; there are several heavy pitches, and one of these bad places, known as the " Big Pitch," is a terror to the river divers, several having been drowned there.

At the time of which I am writing there was no dam at the head of the Falls, but since then one has been built by the enterprising (?) lumbermen who operate on the river above.

These gentlemen are the Goths and Vandals of Northern New England. Every beautiful stream, every pond and lake, every picturesque piece of scenery, is doomed to ruin if there is any lumber in the vicinity.

If the Legislature of Maine was awake to the best interests of the State it would secure a large tract of these wild lands for a public park, before it is too late, and keep them in their original state.

The amount of money left in Maine during a year by the people who visit it for sport and pleasure is largely in excess of that received from the lumbering business. In other words, the sporting and pleasure travel is worth more to the State than its lumbering operations, and some means should be taken to encourage and foster this travel, which is only in its infancy.

Damming the streams, ponds, and lakes, cutting down the forests, and otherwise disfiguring the natural scenery, is a poor way to do it, and a pine or a spruce standing is sometimes worth more than after it has been run through a mill.

And not only the scenery and the forests, but the game has to suffer from lumbering operations. Take a crew composed of from forty to sixty men, many of whom spend their Sundays in hunting, this being the favorite amusement of a large proportion of the men in every camp, and the number of large animals they will kill during the winter would surprise the Fish and Game Commissioners of the State if they knew it. And a large part of this game is killed in the close season, when the snows are so deep that it is difficult for a moose, deer, or caribou to escape the hunter, who always travels on snow-shoes.

The interest I feel in my subject, and which I am sure a majority of my readers share, has made me digress from my story, and, without further argument, I return to it, only adding that what I have said of Maine is just as applicable to New Hampshire.

At the Berlin Mills House Mr. Brown had told us that the Company had four boats at the landing, and that we could take either one of them, and described them to me carefully.

We found six or seven boats at the landing, but they were all heavy but one. Some of them also were deficient in oars and rowlocks, and when I fortunately stumbled upon a light "Graves" boat, of the Adirondack pattern, I told Jack that he need not spend any more time looking over the boats, for that was the craft for us, and the oars and paddle that belonged to it we found all right underneath. It laid bottom up, and, righting it, we launched it and stowed our things away in it. As Fickett had told me that Mr. Flint owned the boat, and as we were going to his camp and expected to see him up there, I had no hesitation in taking it, although it is a poor plan, generally speaking, to use a boat without permission of the owner.

We were soon afloat, and with Jack at the oars, and I at the paddle, the boat sped up the river rapidly. As we wished to know how long it would take us from the Falls to Flint's Camp, I looked at my watch as we left the landing, and it was just ten o'clock.

To make all the progress possible we agreed to spell each other at the oars every hour. The boat shot swiftly along, the snow fell as fast as ever, the air literally being white with the falling flakes so thickly did they come; and, although they were not as large as clam-shells, they were the largest snow-flakes that I had ever seen.

The air was quite mild, and the snow that fell upon us and into the boat melted about as fast as it struck. As I looked ahead up the river everything was a sheet of snowy white but the dark water over which we were gliding, and the air was so thick with the snow that I could see but a short distance.

A Cold Bite.

At eleven o'clock we reversed places, and I took the oars, and Jack the paddle. Soon after we had changed we passed old Bennet, one of the best guides in the country, and two of his boys, who were camped on the right bank. They hailed us as we went by, and inquired where we were going.

I told them "To Parmachenee," and the old man advised us to turn back, saying that winter had commenced, and that we would get snowed in.

I replied, with a laugh, that I would risk it, and we kept on.

With each mile of our advance, however, we noticed the snow deeper on the banks of the river. It reminded me of Longfellow's lines: —

> "Ever deeper, deeper, deeper,
> Fell the snow o'er all the landscape, —
> Fell the covering snow, and drifted
> Through the forest, round the village."

When we stopped at noon, and went on shore to take our lunch, we found nearly a foot on the ground, and everything completely soaked. Under the circumstances it was hardly worth while making a fire, so we squatted down in the snow, ate a couple of cold biscuits and a piece of meat each, smoked a few moments, and then were ready to go on. Before we started we turned our boat over and emptied out several inches of water that had made from the melting snow.

Jack took the oars, and again we were heading up

the river. I told him not to pull too hard for the present, as we ought to reach the Narrows before his hour was up, and, as the current is very strong there, he would need all his strength.

Nothing could be more disagreeable than such a storm as we were now encountering. The great flakes of snow, swept in our face by little gusts of wind, melted about as soon as they struck, and our clothing was thoroughly soaked, as much so as if it had rained all the time. We did not feel very pleasant, but we obtained a little consolation from watching the trees nearest us as we swept along. Fairly loaded with feathery flakes of dazzling whiteness, they presented a most beautiful appearance.

"I wish it would clear up," growled Jack, after a silence that became unbearable.

"So do I; but you need not look for the sun to-day."

About quarter of one we reached the foot of the Narrows, and stopped a moment to take a look at the water. The river contracts at this point to a few yards in width, running between two ledges. Some people in ascending the river haul their boats up this rapid water by a long rope, one staying in the boat to keep it clear of the rocks, while the others walk along the high bank and tow the boat. This is much the easiest way; but, as we had no rope, we had either to overcome the current, or carry around the swift water, a job we did not like with a foot of snow on the ground.

IN THE NARROWS.

"What do you think of it, Jack?" I asked, as he sat watching the current over his shoulder.

"I think it is pretty quick water, as the Indians say, but I guess we are good for it; say when you are ready."

We backed the boat down a rod or two, to give us a chance to get some speed before we struck the swift part of the current, and then started up again. Oars and paddle were plied with a will; but, as we struck the bottom of the swift water, our speed began to slacken, until, as we neared the upper end, we entirely lost our headway, and in a moment were going down stream like an arrow shot from a bow. We kept the boat straight, however, and, quicker than I can write, we were back to our starting-point.

"By Jove!" cried Jack, as our boat swung around in the eddy at the foot of the rapid, "we won't give it up that way. Let's try it again."

"All right! But, instead of taking long strokes as you did before, try short, sharp ones. I think they are better in quick water."

Backing down again we put on steam in starting, and as the boat's bow struck the quick water we changed our long stroke to short and sharp ones, with a perceptibly better effect. Inch by inch we gained on the current. Now we reached the middle of the passage, and, although the boat had lost some speed, she moved considerably faster than the first time.

"Put her through," cried Jack; "we shall fetch it this time."

And in fact we did, for in a few moments more we had struck the head of the Narrows, and swept on up the river where the stream was wider, and the current not more than one-fourth as strong.

A half mile or so above the Narrows we stopped for five minutes' rest and smoke, and Jack and I changed places. From this point up, the river was much more shallow than below the Narrows, and we came to occasional rips, where we had to push with the oars, the water being too low to row in. We should have made better headway in these places with a setting-pole, but there was none in the boat.

When we reached the Lower Metalluc Pond I had half a mind to stop, and camp overnight, in the hope that we might have better weather the next day.

I proposed it to Jack, but he did not receive it favorably, saying we would be much better off in a good log-camp like Flint's than in any shelter we could build in such a storm.

There are some very pleasant camping spots around this pond, and its outlet is a good place for trout. It is also a favorite resort for ducks, and many are shot there during the fall of each year. Jack suggested that we stop there a day or two, on our return, if the weather was favorable; and, with this understanding, we continued on our way.

About three o'clock we had to go on shore and turn

the water and slush out of the boat again, for the snow was falling as fast as ever. In going through the meadows we were surprised to see a number of robins, and hear them singing as gaily as they would in May. Some of the old guides and hunters, familiar with this part of the country, say that the robins stop around the meadows all winter, and feed on the round wood and other berries that grow in the vicinity.

Along these meadows are some very fine elm-trees, that would be worth a large sum of money for shade-trees, if they grew anywhere near a city. The river through this meadow-land is also very crooked, and as you sweep around some of the sharp turns you obtain, on a clear day, beautiful views of the mountains in the vicinity.

The Upper Metalluc Pond lies a short distance back from the right-hand side of the river, about half-way through the meadows, and is a shoal, marshy pond of several acres in extent. This is also a good place for ducks in the fall, and a favorite resort for parties who visit this wilderness to camp out.

A spotted line runs three miles east to Lincoln Pond, the largest pond contiguous to the Magalloway, into which it empties by means of Lincoln Pond Brook. This sheet of water is about two miles long, surrounded by a dense forest, and offers splendid trout-fishing in the proper season. Small trout are plentiful in it, and we have heard of cases where they were taken weighing from two to six pounds each.

Daylight hung on better than we expected, but everything being covered with a mantle of white we did not look for a very dark night. After leaving the meadows we struck the fir woods again, and the trees were so loaded with snow that you could hardly see a limb. About five o'clock we reached the foot of the Big Rips, and tried to row up them, but we could not do it. Twice we tried it, and twice the current bore us down.

Thinking, however, that we were about as wet as we could be, I told Jack that we would try it once more, and as soon as the boat began to stop we would both jump into the river and wade up the rest of the way. At this time he was rowing and I was using the paddle.

We backed off from the foot of the rapids a short distance, and then started ahead. We plied oars and paddle valiantly, and shot the boat half-way up the incline before she began to waver. As soon as her head-way slackened I went out over the stern, and lit in three feet of water. So rapid was the current that I had to dig my feet into the gravel in order to keep from being swept down. The rocks and pebbles on the bottom were as slippery as glass, and that did not improve our footing much.

Jack struck the water about as soon as I did, and Spot, like a good sailor, followed us; but the current was too much for him, and he was swept down to the foot of the rapids, where he took to the shore, and,

THROUGH THE MEADOWS.

wallowing through the snow, joined us at the head of the Rips.

"How do you like it, Jack?" I cried, as we worked our way slowly up the rapids.

"I have seen warmer water than this," he answered, as he tugged away at the painter, and then muttered to himself something about "Arctic boating."

A moment after this the water suddenly deepened, and in one step Jack went nearly to his arms. This was too much of a good thing, and while I was laughing at the way he went down he climbed into the boat.

Taking the oars he held the boat against the current while I tumbled in, and hauled in the dog, who had swam out to us. Then we went on again, and soon passed the mouth of the little Magalloway, which empties into the main river from the left. This stream was nearly filled up with snow, and it really began to look as if winter was upon us.

A short distance above the Forks we run our boat into a little logon on the left, and, hauling her out, turned her bottom up. Everything was so covered with snow, and it was so dark, that we could not find the regular landing.

Before making a start I sat down on the boat and pulled off my rubber boots, which had extra long legs, coming clear to my hips. I turned the water out of them which I had taken in while climbing up the Big Rips, and Jack laughed at me while I was thus engaged. By wearing these boots I had hoped to keep my feet and legs dry, but one or two unlucky slips, while walking the boat up the rapid, had ruined my precaution, and I laughed in concert with my companion.

ARCTIC BOATING.

CHAPTER VIII.

"Who, when great trials come,
Nor seeks nor shuns them, but doth calmly stay,
Till he the thing and the example weigh." — HERBERT.

OUT OF THE STORM.

"HOW far is it to Sunday Pond Camp, Captain?" asked Jack. "The snow is two feet deep here, and I hope we shall not have to travel in it very far to-night."

"It is about a mile, but the first thing is to find the road."

As Jack had said, the snow was really two feet deep, and it was not a very easy matter getting around in it. We groped our way through the trees for a short distance, then came into a small clearing, and, after hunting around this for fifteen minutes, found the road, and with a gladsome cry struck out for the camp.

As the snow had increased with every mile of our advance northward I judged the storm had swept down from Canada, and wondered how much snow they were getting the other side of the boundary. I learned from the papers after my return home that nearly three feet on a level fell in Quebec during this storm, although it all went off again before winter finally set in.

"How is this for a young winter, Jack?" I screamed, as we wallowed along.

"I call it a pretty good beginning," he replied, and then added, crossly, "If you had taken my advice we shouldn't have been here."

Locomotion was so difficult that much conversation was out of the question.

Our exertions made us puff and pant, and in spite of our best efforts we progressed at a snail's pace. Indeed, we could only go a few rods without stopping to take breath. Our work on the river had been child's play compared with what we were now doing.

We were hungry, wet, and cold, and to add to our discomfort the wind had increased to a gale, and the snow was swept into our faces with a force that nearly blinded us. Indeed we were in great danger of losing the road, or passing the camp without seeing it, and I encouraged the dog to keep ahead, knowing that he would bark if he came within sight or smell of a house.

For half an hour or more we struggled on, now crawling under some large windfall, then climbing over smaller ones, until we were about used up, and we were just thinking of taking our chances where we were, and camping until morning, when in a lull of the wind we heard the dog bark a short distance ahead of us, and, gazing sharply in the direction of the sound, caught the twinkle of a light through the trees.

At that moment our feelings were better imagined than described. We were like the storm-tossed mariner on the mighty ocean, who, after fighting with the storm for hours, and feeling that in a few minutes more his vessel must be a wreck, suddenly discerns the welcome beacon that guides him safely to a harbor.

One long, loud "Hurrah! there's a light; it must be the camp," and the next moment we were pressing forward regardless of wind or snow. The knowledge that we were so near shelter gave us new life and strength, and nerved us up for increased effort. But fortunate it was for us that the distance was so short, for we could not have traveled another mile had our lives depended upon it. A few moments more and we had reached the building, and were sheltered beneath its hospitable roof.

We found two hunters there who had been setting a line of traps between Parmachenee and Connecticut Lakes, and who were stopping in the camp until the storm was over. One of them, whose name was Morton, told us that Flint had gone to Bethel, and would not be back for two weeks, so that we should not see him. This was a disappointment; but it was in keeping with the luck that had followed us from the start.

Morton asked me if we were hungry, and I told him we had only had a lunch since breakfast.

"And it is seven o'clock now," he said; "get off your wet things, and I will get you some supper while you dry your clothes."

The other fellow, whom I will call Dick, went out and brought in two or three armfuls of wood, and in a short time the large stove in the kitchen was red-hot, and Jack and I, who stood as near to it as the heat would allow, were enveloped in clouds of steam sent forth from our wet garments.

In about half an hour Morton announced that supper was ready, and we sat down to the table, on which we found hot biscuit, fried trout and pork, potatoes, cold corned beef (canned), and some currant jelly. We were as hungry as sharks, and I thought we should never get done eating; but finally, with an effort, I tore myself away from the table, and told Jack I had my opinion of any man who could eat longer than myself.

"You can't shame me any," replied Jack, with a laugh, scooping in the one remaining biscuit; "after what we've been through to-day I intend to eat until I get filled up."

"That's right," declared Norton. "Don't let the captain bluff you. Have another cup of tea, Jack?"

"Thanks; don't care if I do, seeing it's you;" and the unblushing fellow passed his empty cup to be filled for the third time.

"Great Jerusalem, Jack! I hope I shall not have to sleep with you to-night. Unless your digestion is

A Welcome Sight.

better than most people's, you will be dreaming of panthers and bob-cats, and kick me out of bed."

"Don't worry, Cap," laughed Dick; "you can each have a bed to yourself."

After we had appeased our hunger we gathered around the stove, and Jack and I finished the drying-off process. We sat and smoked and talked until about ten o'clock. Morton and his partner, and Jack and I exchanged experiences, and we passed a very pleasant evening. Morton thought we had made the quickest time on record, in coming from the Magalloway settlement to Sunday Pond in ten hours.

"We did not hurry much," I told him, "and I think we could beat our time of to-day in pleasant weather."

"You would have to 'hump her' some to do it," remarked Dick.

"We'll make better time going down, see if we don't," said Jack.

"Have you seen any moose about here, Morton?" I asked.

"Not yet; but we saw the tracks of a thundering big one yesterday. We intended to have gone out for him to-day, but this snow spoiled our sport,— covered his trail up. But we intend to shoot one before we leave."

"I would give five dollars to get a shot at one," declared Jack, his eyes sparkling with excitement.

"You can go out with us some day," said Morton.

"I know about where to look for them, and we can track them easily now, there is so much snow."

"But a fellow would need snow-shoes," returned Jack. "There would not be much fun in hunting only in boots, with two or three feet of snow on the ground."

"There are plenty of snow-shoes here. Did you ever use them?" Morton asked this question with a smile.

"Many a time," replied Jack. "I have done a good deal of snow-shoeing around the Richardson Lakes. I chased a deer last winter over a mountain at the lower end of Lake Welokennebacook, and shot him about three miles from where I first discovered him. The crust was not heavy enough to hold him or he would have given me the lurch. He was a very large buck, and weighed a hundred and fifty pounds."

"That is a pretty large deer," said Morton. "By the way we'll give you some venison for breakfast. We have one hind quarter left of a buck we shot last week over at the foot of Bose-Buck Mountain. How long do you think you will stay up here, Captain?"

"That depends upon circumstances," I replied. "But we shall have to get back to the Brown Farm by next Friday noon at the latest, as the steamer makes her last trip on that day for the season."

"We could hire a boat at the Brown Farm and row down to Upton," suggested Jack.

"Yes; but how would we get the boat back?" I returned.

"I did not think of that."

"We could walk from the Brown Farm down to Errol, and then get a team to take us to Upton by the way of Cambridge; but it would not pay for us to take that trouble and expense unless we are going to strike pretty good hunting up here."

"There's always plenty of hunting up here," remarked Dick, smiling at me; "but the amount of game you find is another thing."

"Well, there's fun in hunting, whether you shoot anything or not," returned Jack.

I asked Morton what he thought about the weather, and he said his opinion was that it would clear off cold, and that we would not see bare ground again until next spring. Dick thought also that winter had set in, and "reckoned" that the rivers would freeze up as soon as it was through snowing.

I was sorry to hear these men talk in the way they did, because, if their predictions were to be verified, it was evident to me that the sooner Jack and I left for the settlement, the better, without stopping for any sport.

We were not prepared to stay in the woods during winter weather, and had counted on the next two or three weeks being warm and pleasant, when we started on our trip. Neither did we care to break ice on the river if it froze up, and we were in duty bound to return the boat we had come up in to the place where we had taken it from. Therefore I went to bed feeling rather blue, and laid awake for some time thinking what was best to be done, but finally fell off into a doze without coming to any conclusion.

I had slept but a short time when I was awakened by a tremendous crash, and a trembling of the camp; it seemed to me as if the building was coming down around our ears. Every one was on his feet in a moment, anxiously inquiring what was the trouble. Morton lit a lantern and I opened the door, and we all peered out. We found that a large spruce that stood near the camp had been blown down, and in its fall had just grazed the corner of the camp, knocking off some of the shingles, but not doing any further damage.

Before we closed the door we heard another frightful crash but a short distance away, marking the death of another forest monarch. The wind had hauled around to the north-west, and was blowing with a fury that I never saw surpassed. It was only one o'clock, but not knowing what might happen, for there were a number of large spruces standing near the building, we all dressed, and laid down on the outside of the bed, so as to be able to leave in a moment if necessary.

After dressing I lay awake about an hour, listening to the roar of the wind as it howled through the forest, and the crashing of trees as they fell to the ground, some of them, as we found next day, being torn up by the roots. I finally sank into a troubled sleep, during which I dreamed that the steamer had broken from her moorings and had gone ashore. It was seven o'clock when I awoke, and I could hear the voices of the others in the kitchen.

I jumped up and pulled on my boots, then went out and washed. I found Dick and Jack getting breakfast, and the savory smell of broiled venison filled the kitchen. About eight o'clock we sat down to the table. After breakfast Morton and I washed up the dishes and cleared away; then we all sat down for a smoke and a chat.

The wind had entirely ceased, and the snow had stopped falling, but as yet it did not look anything like clearing off.

"Is it not unusual," I asked of Morton, "to have such a big storm as this so early in the season?"

"I don't know as I ever saw quite as much snow as this the second week in October. But we generally get snow-squalls here by the last of September, and more or less after that until the following June."

"I should hate to live in this country then, for I despise snow."

"If you wish to hate yourself," said Dick, "you orter live in a loggin' camp up here one winter. I've seen it snow every day for a month."

"Oh, get out!" I replied, laughing; "a person could not get around in such a storm."

"I don't mean that it snowed hard every day, but that there wasn't a day for a month but what it snowed.

Some days there wouldn't be a quarter of an inch fall, and some days it would spit snow all day while the sun was shining."

"How long do you fellows intend to stop here?" queried Jack.

"We shall leave here as soon as the storm is over, and go back to Connecticut Lake," replied Morton, "and shall probably stay there until January. But it will depend some on the weather and our luck in trapping."

"Have you a good camp at Connecticut Lake?" I inquired.

"First-rate," said Dick, "you had better go over there with us."

"If this snow had not come I had intended to go over there and stay one or two nights, but, as it is, I think I am far enough from the settlements."

"I wish you could have gone over, Captain," remarked Morton. "I have the head of a moose and a caribou's head set up at the camp, and I should like to have had you seen them."

"I have no doubt they are worth looking at, but I am not likely to get a look at them this trip."

"Was the moose a large one?" questioned Jack.

"I should think he'd weigh a thousand pounds," declared Dick. "It was a bull moose, and we put five bullets into him before we killed him."

"Where did you shoot him?" I asked.

"Between Second and Third Lakes," replied Morton.

"Is there any reading-matter around this shanty?" I inquired, looking at the two hunters.

"You may find some old papers," said Morton, and then, with a laugh, added, "They haven't started a public library in this country yet, Captain."

"I suppose not. But I should want them to if I had to stay here. I wouldn't live here through the winter for a thousand dollars a month, unless I could have plenty of books and cigars;" and I took the old papers that Dick had found and began looking them over.

Jack, not caring to read, borrowed a fishing-rod from Morton, and went down to the pond, a few rods away, to see if he could capture a trout.

I smiled when I saw him go out, for it was so cold and blustering I knew he would not stay long.

In half an hour or so he came back, declaring that he was half frozen, and without a single fish. He drew up to the stove, pulled off his boots, and placed his feet in the oven, and began growling about the trout not biting.

"That is all right," remarked Dick, laughing. "It's Sunday. Fish don't bite up in this country Sundays."

"Nor week days either, such weather as this," returned Jack.

"I'll go fishing with you to-morrow, and take you where you can get some trout."

"I don't believe you will unless the weather changes. If it holds on like this we'll be sliding down river to-morrow;" and Jack looked to me to corroborate his assertion.

"I think that will be the wisest plan, for we can't have any fun here as things are now."

Just then Jack gave a howl, and pushed back from the stove with such violence that his chair upset, and over he went. He was on his feet in a moment, and gave the chair a kick that sent it spinning across the room, and then began rubbing his left foot.

As soon as we could stop laughing, for his whole action was exceedingly comical, Morton asked him what the matter was.

"Burned my foot; and it's nothing to laugh at," he added savagely.

As he was evidently not in a mood for joking I returned to my reading, and Morton and Dick went out for water and wood, and we let Jack alone until he recovered his temper, which had been sadly marred by his accident.

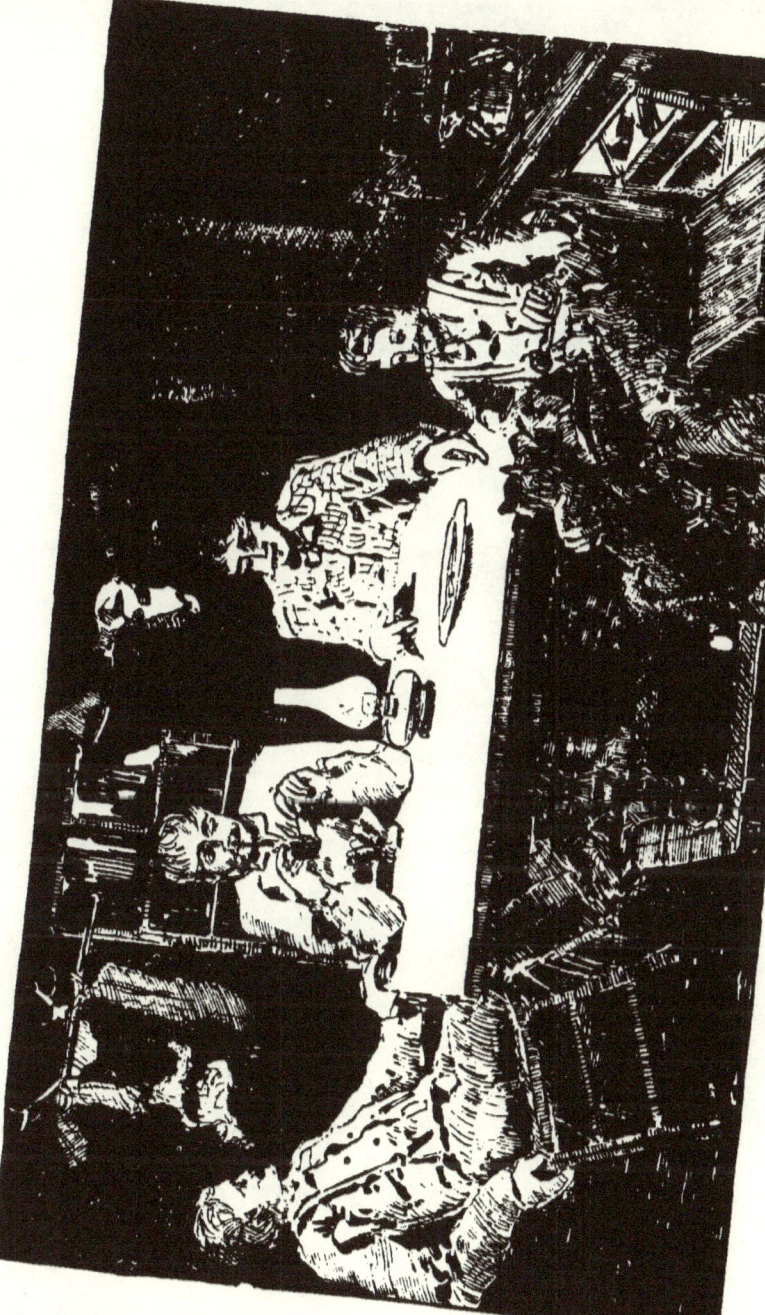

In Camp.

CHAPTER IX.

*"This brings a tale into my mind,
Which, if you are not disinclined
To listen, I will now relate."* — LONGFELLOW.

A QUIET SUNDAY.

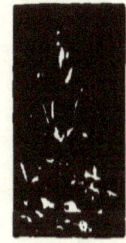MISERY likes company, and about ten o'clock who should walk into the camp but Fred Parker! We were glad to see him. He stared with astonishment when he saw Jack and I, and wanted to know where we came from. I told him, and asked him what he was doing. He said he was trapping with John Canforth, and that they had a camp up at the outlet of Parmachenee, and wanted Jack and I to be sure to come and see them before we went down river, which we promised to do. Fred stopped until nearly noon, and then went off to his own camp.

After dinner I asked Jack if he was going to church.

"To church? Well, I declare, it is Sunday, isn't it? I had forgot all about it. If we go to any church I guess it will be Mr. Woods'. Suppose we take a walk up to the lake."

I was agreeable; so, putting on our overcoats, for it was much colder than the day before, we went out and struck for the lake.

We found it slow, tiresome walking, and we were an hour and a half in covering the three miles between the camp and the lake. On every side we saw the effects of the terrible tempest of the night before. Large and tall spruces, huge yellow birches, and other trees lay prostrate in every direction; some twisted up by the roots, others broken off five or six feet from the ground, and I felt thankful that we had passed through the night safely.

The clouds were so low that all the hills and mountains about the lake were enveloped in mist, and after watching the water break up on the shore a short time we followed the lake around to the outlet, and went down to the dam, near which was Canforth's Camp. We wallowed through the snow to the camp and went in, and found both Fred and John at home.

We stopped there awhile spinning yarns, and talked with them about their trapping. They were discouraged with the heavy fall of snow, as they had a line of traps set about twenty miles long, and they would have a nice job visiting them and digging them out.

Fred wanted to know how long we were going to stay, and I informed him that unless it cleared up that night we should go down river the next day, for there was no fun stopping where we were with two feet of snow on the ground; and, besides, if the river froze up it would be bad for us to get the boat back.

"Have you taken much fur, John?" inquired Jack.

"Not a great deal. We have about a dozen skins. We haven't fairly begun business yet, and this storm has upset some of our calculations."

"How long are you going to stay, Fred?" I inquired.

"Until the first of January, if the pork and beans hold out."

"How about the venison, Fred?" said Jack.

"Oh, there's plenty of that around here on the hoof. We intend to sample some before long."

"I should like to stay here a month," asserted Jack, "and see if I could not kill a moose."

"So should I; but it don't look as if we would this trip;" and I glanced out at the dark and sullen sky.

"Where did you leave your boat, Captain?" inquired Fred.

"At the mouth of the river below the Upper Dam," I returned. "Do you think it is a good place?"

"First-rate," he replied. "The water never freezes there, — the current is too strong."

"Have you any gum around the camp, Fred?" inquired Jack.

"Not a bit. We haven't been gumming yet, but intend to get a lot to take down with us before we leave."

"Never mind," replied Jack, with a smile, as he took a chew of tobacco; "this is better."

We stopped with the hunters until nearly dark, and then we returned to our camp. We had a good supper, and then gathered around the fire, and listened to stories from our two companions, who seemed to have passed through many exciting experiences by field and flood. One of the stories that Dick related I quote in his own words as near as possible.

"Three years ago," began Dick, as he settled himself comfortably in his chair, and took an extra pull at his pipe, "I came over here about the first of November, from Pittsburg, on a hunting trip. I had about sixty pounds of traps, twenty-five of grub, and my rifle, besides a frying-pan, pair of blankets, and a tin teapot.

"The next morning after my arrival here I met an explorer who had been looking out loggin' chances, and who had come across the country from the Seven Ponds. He told me game was very thick over there, and that there were two families of beaver in the vicinity, and said I could do a big fall's business trapping in that vicinity.

"As I had never been farther east than Parmachence Lake I asked him a good many questions about the country, and whether it would be hard getting there.

"He assured me that an experienced woodsman would have no trouble in making the trip, and, as I always carried a compass in the woods, I obtained some points from him to travel by.

A QUIET SUNDAY. 149

"His account of the country pleased me so much that I determined to try it, for if I could bring back a good pack of beaver-skins it would pay me well for my trouble, and I started eastward that very afternoon, and camped that night on the bank of the Cupsuptic River.

"It was a beautiful day when I started, — a little cool, but clear and bright sunshine, and no snow had as yet fallen to lay on the ground more than a few hours.

"I built a rough bough camp for shelter during the night, and then cutting a small pole I hitched on a fishing-line, and going up the river a few rods caught half-a-dozen small trout. These, with a slice of pork, a couple of slap-jacks that I cooked in the spider, and a pot of hot tea, made a supper good enough for any woodsman, or a city fellow either, if he was as hungry as I.

"After my supper I cut up a huge pile of wood, and made a rousing fire in front of the camp; then spreading some cedar boughs that I had cut when I built the camp, I lay down on them, feet to the fire, pulled my blankets over me, and soon fell asleep.

"It must have been well along towards morning when I awoke, with a stream of water pouring into my face. I sat up for a moment rather bewildered, but soon gathered enough of my wits to see that the rain was pouring in torrents; that my fire was about out, and that the roof of my camp, which had not been built for wet weather, was leaking in fifty places. It was darker than a stack of black cats, and as I arose to my feet I could not see two yards away from me.

"I had camped near several large white birches, and to them I now groped my way, and with my hunting-knife cut off an armful of bark, and then got back to the camp and threw this on the fire with what fuel I had left.

"This soon blazed up, and I could see a short distance around me. I had covered up my flour, which was the only article of food I had with me, that the rain would spoil, the night before, and, examining it, found it to be dry. Recovering it I took my axe, and cut off several large slabs from an old "down" pine near me, which was dry inside, and threw on the fire; then, as I could do nothing more, I sat down near the fire, pulled my blankets over my head, and waited for daylight.

"It came slowly enough, and after light I anxiously looked at the sky for some signs of fair weather; but it seemed a hopeless case. My blankets by this time were wet through, and I spread them on top of the camp in the hope that they would keep a little of the water out of it.

"There was not a breath of wind, and the weather had moderated a good deal, it being much warmer than the day before.

"While getting my breakfast I came to the sensible conclusion of staying where I was until the rain stopped, and, after I had eaten, I walked up the bank of the river a short distance, and finding signs of game went back to camp for a couple of traps, and these I set in hopes of getting a fisher or an otter. Deer-tracks were also plenty along the river, and, while I had not caught sight of any, I was in hopes to during the day, and kept my rifle loaded and under cover ready for immediate use.

"At noon it rained as hard as ever, and after dinner I cut up a lot of white birch, and about half of the old dead pine, and 'sacked' it to camp. Then I lit my pipe, took my rifle, and went down river about a mile. On my way back I started up two partridges, and shot one of them. I hunted for the other, but could not find it. The one I shot, however, made me a good supper, and I felt thankful for that.

" By dark the river had risen over four feet, and was now a raging torrent. But as there was a narrow place in it just above my camp, where I could bridge it by falling a sapling pine, I did not borrow any trouble on that account.

" At seven o'clock the rain was falling as hard as ever, and I began to entertain thoughts of another flood, and wondered if I hadn't better build an ark. I was wet through to my skin, with no present prospect of getting dry, and I concluded to sit up all night rather than lie down so wet. I thought best to stir around once in a while, as I had no liquor with me, and in fact I never use it."

" You're a sensible man," I remarked.

He smiled, and continued : " About nine o'clock the

rain stopped as suddenly as it commenced. The fire ceased sputtering, and sent out a generous blaze, and I made an effort to dry my clothing, in which I partially succeeded, and at midnight I turned in, after putting a lot of wood on the fire.

"It was six o'clock when I woke, and I was all of a shiver. The wind was beginning to blow a little, and it was very much colder. I stirred around briskly, and after eating my breakfast I went to my traps and found a fisher in one of them. I killed him and carried him and the traps to camp. Then I took off his pelt and stretched it, and then, putting more fuel on the fire, spread my blankets and made a business of drying them.

"By ten o'clock they were dry, and, packing up, I started on. The sun had been shining for an hour or two, but was covered by clouds when I broke camp, and that was the last I saw of it for several days. I crossed the river on a bridge of my own making, and then, taking out my compass, struck out on a northeast course.

"At noon I stopped and built a fire, had dinner, with some hot tea, and then took up my line of march again. Although I had been plenty warm traveling, I found it awful cold when I stopped for dinner, and made up my mind that ice would make that night.

"During the afternoon I put my best foot forward as the saying is, until three o'clock, when I halted and built a camp. It was still cloudy, and looked like snow, and I paid more attention to the construction of this camp than I did to the former one, and made it warmer and tighter.

"After finishing the camp, and cutting a pile of wood for the night, I had my supper, puffed away at my pipe for a while, and then bunked down early.

"I was very tired and dropped asleep in a few moments, and when I awoke it was daylight, and a foot of snow covered the ground, and it was coming down as fast as I ever saw it in my life. I thought this was hard luck, for I had hoped to reach the ponds, and get a good log-camp built before getting much snow. But this was evidently going to be a big storm, and I had got to make the best of it.

"The wind blew quite hard, and had drifted a lot of snow into the camp, and the first thing I did was to remove this, and then fix the front of the camp so it would keep the most of the snow out, and by the aid of one of my blankets I succeeded in doing it. Then I cooked my breakfast and melted some snow for water, for there was no stream near me. While eating I thought if I was going to get 'snowed in' I had better have plenty of fuel on hand, and I cut wood until the cravings of hunger warned me that it must be dinner-time, and, looking at my watch, I found it was one o'clock. I was not over a hundred feet from camp, and it did not take me long to return and get my dinner.

"In the afternoon I brought the wood to camp and piled it near. While I was cooking my supper I heard a noise just behind the camp, and, catching up my rifle, I wallowed toward the sound, for the snow was now three feet deep, and caught sight of a deer as he passed across a glimmer of my camp-fire.

"I shot quick, but took careful aim, and the deer, after a jump or two, fell. When I reached him he was dead, and I found that it was an old buck, that would weigh a hundred and fifty or sixty pounds. I cut his throat, and, dragging him up to camp, hung him to a tree and let him bleed."

"That was a lucky shot," said Jack.

"Yes, in more ways than one; for, if I was obliged to travel in three or four feet of snow, I would need snow-shoes, and I had brought none with me. The deer's flesh would furnish me with an abundance of fresh meat, and his hide with material for my snow-shoes, the frames of which I could make from some hard-wood tree.

"I thought a fresh venison steak would not be bad for supper, and more to my liking than salt pork, of which I had only a pound or two, and, suspending my cooking, I took the hide off the deer, cut him open, removed his entrails, and hung up the four quarters, after cutting two generous slices from one of the hind ones.

"In spite of the blinding snow-storm that still continued I did not fret, for I now felt that I was pretty well fixed, and after a comfortable smoke I turned in, hoping that the snow would stop during the night. I am a sound sleeper, and I had, probably, lost all consciousness before I had laid down fifteen minutes.

" When I awoke I found myself lying on my face, my hands thrown behind me over my back, and I felt a heavy pressure on my body. I thought at first I was not really awake, but was the victim of nightmare. This idea soon passed away when I heard noises of grunts and hard breathing, and realized that some one had bound my hands, and was engaged in tying my feet."

" That must have been a pleasant awakening," I suggested.

" Very," he replied, in a slightly sarcastic tone, and then resumed his story.

" I had no idea, of course, who the men were, or what they were treating me in such a manner for, but I did not propose to lay still and take it, and I began to struggle, and tried to kick. But before I could accomplish anything I received a clout over the head that made me unconscious.

" When I returned to my senses it was daylight, and I could see, outside, my two captors, who, from their talk and appearance, I soon found were Canadian Indians. They talked mostly in French, which I did not understand, and were cooking some of my deer-meat.

" I hailed them, but beyond looking at me once they paid me no further attention. After they were through eating, the largest one, a very powerful fellow, came in and examined my bonds. I asked him for some breakfast, but he did not let on that he heard me.

"They began to busy themselves about something at once, and after a while I could see that they were making snow-shoes. They had cut up the deer's hide into thongs, and had obtained some wood for frames near the camp, which they were fashioning into shape.

"They worked very rapidly, and about eleven o'clock had finished the two pair, and then prepared to depart. They paid me a farewell visit before they left, and robbed me of my watch, pocket compass, matches, and in fact everything I had about me. They could not have cleaned me out more thoroughly if they had been city footpads. It is needless, perhaps, to tell you that my rifle, frying-pan, blankets, and everything else went with them, and I cursed them savagely, and only wished that I could shoot them; and I would have done it with as little compunction as I would have shot a rat."

"Served them right," echoed Jack.

"It strikes me that you were in a bad plight," I remarked.

"Bad! I should say so. As soon as the villains were out of hearing I began to try and loosen my hands. Fortunately for me they had bound me with some of the thongs of the deer-skin, and, as it was very pliable, I succeeded, after half an hour's work, in freeing my hands, and after that soon had the bands off my feet. When I stood upright I came near falling down I was so stiff and numb, but after a step or two my blood began to circulate, and I found I could get around all right.

"I was as hungry as a wolf, and I found one of the fore-quarters of the deer hanging where I had left it. The rest they had taken with them, and only left this, I suppose, because they could not carry it. They had played me another mean trick by putting out the fire, but luckily I found a few matches in an inner pocket of my hunting-shirt, and, although they were damp, I succeeded in lighting one after spoiling about half of them. I soon had a fire going, and tearing off a piece of the deer-meat by means of a stick, for I had no knife to cut it, I pushed a small maple limb through it, and held it over the fire until it was roasted. I had to eat it without salt, as the villains had taken every crumb I had brought.

"While eating I finally came to the determination of making my way back to Parmachenee Lake in the least possible time. Several different projects suggested themselves to me, but I cast them aside one by one as impracticable, and as soon as I had appeased my hunger I took a look at the sun, which was now shining brightly, and grasping the remains of my venison, which was all the scoundrels had left me to take away, I struck a bee-line for the west, in hopes of reaching some of the lumber camps on the Magalloway, above Parmachenee.

"I found it wearisome work wallowing through the

snow, which varied in depth from three to four feet, but as I had no load but my venison, to which I clung with an energy that would have made a spectator laugh, I made very fair progress. I stopped for the night in a group of windfalls, made a fire, supped on my venison, but could not sleep on account of the cold, and amused myself by keeping up the fire.

"With the first streak of dawn I cooked some more of the venison, ate it, and continued my tramp. About noon, as near as I could judge by the sun, I reached the Cupsuptic once more, and found a favorable place to cross, the water being but a few inches deep, the freshet having subsided. When I had crossed the river I started a fire, and roasted what was left of the venison. I was not very particular about the cooking, for daylight was valuable, and I ate the meat pretty rare. Then I took a drink from the river and pushed on for the Magalloway.

"I was in hopes to reach it that night; but I never should have done it if luck had not been on my side. About half an hour before dark I heard the blows of an axe resounding through the woods, and, heading for the sound, came upon a chopper who had just finished his day's work, and was starting for the camp. I told him my story in as few words as possible, and in his company soon reached a sled-road, and, following this, a half-hour brought us to camp. In the crew were some men that I was acquainted with, and they gave me a warm welcome, and after supper, which tasted particularly good that night, I saw the boss and engaged myself to him for the winter, and chopped, instead of trapping."

"That was a rough adventure," remarked Jack, as he knocked the ashes out of his pipe.

"You bet it was," added Dick.

"And did you never see the thieves since?" I asked, as I arose, preparatory to going to bed.

"Not a sign of them. I would like to meet them by daylight with a rifle in my hand, and I would put my mark on them."

"I declare it is eleven o'clock," I said, looking at my watch. "I must go to bed."

"I guess we had better follow suit," chimed in Morton, as he began putting out the lights.

The interest I had taken in Dick's narrative had kept me wide awake while he was talking, but as I began undressing I realized that I was outrageously sleepy, and I had no sooner struck the bed than I became oblivious to all my surroundings.

Whether I had eaten something for supper that night that caused rebellion in my stomach I did not know, but of one thing I was certain, and that was that I did not sleep well, for in a short time — I judged about an hour — I awoke trembling in every limb, and my body bathed in perspiration.

I had been dreaming of the steamer, and thought that she had sunk while I was in the cabin, and my extraordinary struggles to free myself, that I might rise to the surface of the lake, and make some effort to reach the shore, were probably the cause of my sweating and trembling.

I sat up in bed a few moments to collect my thoughts, but the air in the house was so chilly that I was glad to crawl under the bedclothes again in a very few seconds.

I thought to myself this is the second time I have dreamed of the steamer being wrecked; I do hope that she rode out the gale in safety.

I lay awake for some time worrying over the boat, but finally dropped to sleep again; but I awoke several times before daylight, and always with the impression that the steamer was in trouble.

CHAPTER X.

"It may be that these fragments owe alone
To the fair setting of their circumstances —
The associations of time, scene, and audience —
Their place amid the pictures which fill up
The chambers of my memory." — WHITTIER.

WE RETRACE OUR COURSE.

WE arose the next morning, hoping to find it warm and pleasant, but the day presented the same appearance as its predecessor, — fog thick and low, with but slight change in the temperature.

Fred came down to the camp in the middle of the forenoon, and said he believed we should have more snow, and advised us to go home unless we were prepared to stay three or four weeks.

With the present state of the weather I had no intention of doing that; if the sun had been shining bright and clear, with some prospect of the snow going off, we should have stopped; but two feet of snow in October was all I wanted to see, and we put everything in readiness for a start.

"I declare," said Morton, as we sat smoking, "I

hate to have you go. If you could hold on two or three days longer you might carry home some venison."

"That is a great temptation," I acknowledged; "but yet I don't think I will venture to stay; first, on account of the weather, and, secondly, on account of the steamer."

"I won't deny that the weather is doubtful; but I don't believe the gale injured your boat any, secured as you say she was."

"It may be foolish on my part, but I can't help thinking she was damaged in that gale. I dreamed again last night that she sank."

"Oh, nonsense!" cried Jack, sending forth several upward curling rings of smoke from his mouth. "The fact is, Captain, you are thinking about the boat all the time. If you did not let your mind run on it so much you would not be troubled by so many doubts and misgivings. Likely enough the gale didn't reach down there at all."

"I know better," I replied; "such a gale of wind as that, a north-wester too, would surely have reached that distance. Why, it is not more than twenty miles in an air-line."

"It might have partially blown itself out before it reached there," suggested Morton. "Perhaps it did not blow more than half as hard there as it did here."

My companions tried to discourage my blue feelings, but did not succeed; but, as the subject was not a pleasant one, I did not pursue it any farther.

HOMEWARD BOUND.

We had an early dinner, and bidding good-by to our friends, made our way to where we had left our boat. We found her well buried in snow, but soon had her all right and in the water. We put in our things, and between twelve and one started down the river. I gave a turn or two of the paddle, and we had reached the middle of the stream, and with the current in our favor we made good head-way. We soon passed the little Magalloway, now so buried in snow that you could scarcely tell where it was, and a few minutes later were shooting the Big Rips, which we found an easier job than forcing our way up.

"It's a little more like fun to come down these rapids," said Jack. "I tell you what, Captain, I shall never forget the chill that water gave me when I struck it. Great snakes! wasn't it cold!"

"Decidedly chilly, Jack; but how would you have liked taking a bath in it?" and I looked at my companion with a smile.

"Do you mean naked?"

"Certainly, in Father Adam's original costume, excepting the fig-leaves."

"None of it for me. Do you take me for a Lap or a Greenlander?"

"I have read of people cutting holes through the ice in winter, and plunging naked into the water for fun. They thought it a nice way of taking a bath."

"Didn't they freeze?" queried Jack, looking at me as if I had been spinning a tough yarn.

"Not a bit of it."

"It's a pity they hadn't," cried Jack, with disgust.

The country presented a strange appearance as we made our way rapidly along: the dark lane of water before us, the white shores on either side, and, overhead, a gray blanket of mist, which was not more than ten or twelve feet above us. The tops of ordinary trees were lost in it, and it seemed as if some immense scythe had levelled the forest to a regular height. There was no wind, so we did not get the beautiful pictures that one sometimes gets when the fog is rapidly dissolved by a steady blow.

Once or twice we passed small birds, that gave voice to a few sweet notes as we floated by, as if astonished to meet a human biped at such a time. Jack said they were snow-birds, and said they had good courage to be out in such weather.

"Let me row now, Jack," I said, after my companion had pulled several miles; "I don't want you to row all the way down river."

"Keep your seat, Captain; I am doing well. I am not tired a bit. Pulling down river and pulling up are two very different things. Just watch the banks and see how we slide along!"

"I have noticed several times that we are making good head-way. But you need not do all the rowing on that account."

"Don't fret, Captain, as long as I don't kick. I am not so bashful but what I will let you know when I am tired."

Just then we turned one of the sharp curves of the river, and I saw a blue heron standing on one leg, on the right-hand bank of the river, close to the water's edge.

"Look at that blue heron, Jack," I whispered, "standing on one foot. I believe he is warming the other one."

Jack ceased rowing, and, turning, took a look at the bird.

"I guess the old fellow is asleep," said Jack, softly. "I'll wake him up."

He reached for his gun, which I handed him; but, just as he was bringing it to his shoulder, the heron gave a startled cry, and, flapping his huge wings, sailed away into the fog.

"By gracious!" cried Jack, with a laugh, as he passed me back his gun, "he'll get lost if he doesn't carry a compass."

The conceit was an odd one, and I joined my companion in his laughter. This aroused Spot from a comfortable nap he had been taking between my legs, and, thinking he must make his share of the noise, he began barking.

"Keep quiet, Spot! Don't let him bark, Captain. We may possibly see a deer along here somewhere."

I quieted the dog, and began to watch the banks of the river more closely. If there were any deer in the neighborhood I was anxious to get a look at them, if nothing more; and, as it was now the open season for large game, we could carry the venison home if we could only get it. Always "catch your eel before you skin it," you know.

"Do you suppose deer travel about much, Jack, when the ground is covered with nearly two feet of snow?"

"Do I? Of course. This snow isn't deep enough to trouble them any, and they have to forage for their living anyhow. Later on, when the snow is four or five feet deep, they get together in 'yards,' if the crust is not strong enough to hold them."

"Did you ever run across a deer-yard?"

"No; but I know a fellow who worked in the woods two winters ago, and he told me that he and three of the crew were out one Sunday toward spring, and they came across a yard where there were nine deer, and they killed the whole of them, and they had fresh meat in camp for a couple of weeks."

"But that was slaughter, Jack. Those fellows ought to have been horsewhipped. It was in the close season, too."

"What do you suppose a logging crew care about close or open season? All they wanted was the fresh meat, and they didn't care how they got it."

A little while before reaching the head of the meadows, as we turned a sharp bend, I was startled by seeing a caribou crossing the river, about twenty rods in advance of us.

"Jack," I cried, "there is a caribou crossing the river just ahead of us."

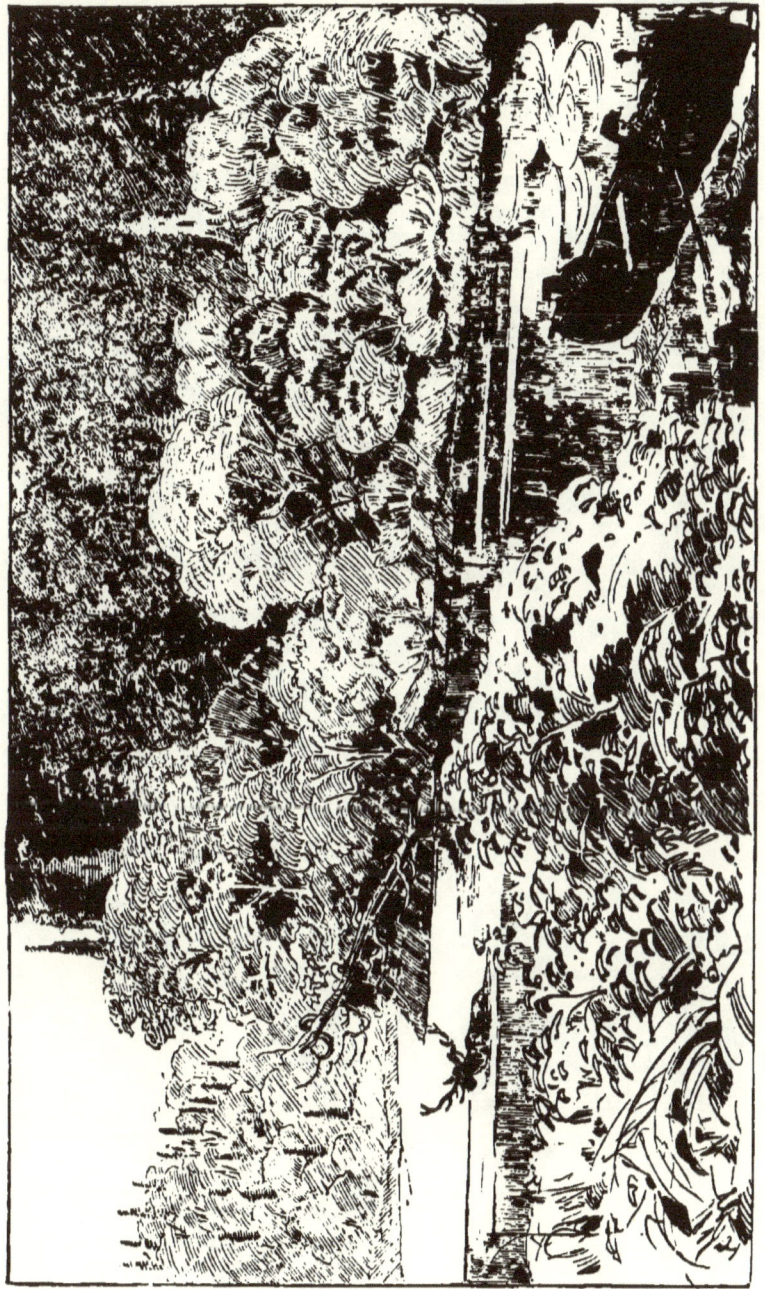
A Caribou Chase.

My companion dropped his oars, which swung in to the side of the boat, and, turning his head, took a glance at the animal.

"Here, take your gun," I urged, passing him the weapon, "and shoot quick!"

Jack grabbed his gun and blazed away at him, and I let drive with my revolver, but, instead of dropping, he bounded off into the woods as if a pack of wolves were after him.

"We didn't hit him," said Jack; "and if I had it wouldn't have done much damage, for I had duck-shot in both barrels."

"Great Christmas!" I exclaimed, thoroughly mad for a moment. "Why didn't you load one barrel, at least, with buck-shot?"

"I don't know why I didn't," answered my companion, looking disgusted at our poor success. "I guess it was absence of mind."

"We will not stop to argue the matter now. Take to the oars and let's get on shore;" and I turned the boat toward the left side of the river.

"Perhaps he won't run far," suggested Jack, as he grasped the oars.

"So far that we shall not get another squint at him, I am afraid."

We ran the boat in on the bank, landing where the caribou took to the woods, and followed his trail for some distance.

We saw several spots of blood along the way, which

showed that we must have hit him, and probably the bullet from my revolver pierced his skin. At any rate I claimed the honor of having wounded him, and, for a wonder, Jack for once "acknowledged the coin."

Jack, who had loaded his gun with buck-shot, as we followed on the trail of the caribou, was very anxious to get another sight of the animal; but, when we had wallowed through the snow for half a mile without coming in sight of the game, became reconciled to giving up the chase, and the print of his hoofs in the snow was the last we saw of Mr. Caribou. Reluctantly we tramped back to the boat, and when we reached the bank of the river found that, through excitement or carelessness, we had not pulled our boat far enough out of the water, and that she had gone adrift in our absence.

With muttered imprecations on our ill luck we turned down river, and waded through the snow along the bank, looking with eager eyes for the boat.

Every little while we would trip over some old log or windfall, which, covered by the snow, made a trap for the unwary, and, losing our balance, we would generally get a snow-bath before we could recover our equilibrium.

This unexpected tramp, with our chase after the caribou, began to tire us, and we hoped each minute would bring us in sight of the boat.

We walked, however, fully half a mile before we found it, and then, to our dismay, saw it on the opposite side of the river, where its farther progress had been checked by a tree which had fallen into the river, but whose roots were still fastened to the bank.

We looked at the boat, and then looked at each other. The question was, how to cross the river.

I broke down a small dead fir, five or six feet long, and, stepping to the water's edge, sounded with it as far out as I could reach, and could not touch bottom. It was very evident we could not get over where we were.

"If I only had the axe," said Jack, "I would cut one of those large spruces," — nodding toward a group of trees, ten or a dozen feet away, — "and bridge the river."

"As you don't happen to have it," I returned, cheerfully, "I shall have to go back to that last set of rips we passed, and try and cross there. I don't think the water is over a foot deep there. You walk down to that point just ahead of you, and I will bring the boat down there and take you in."

"All right, Captain; but be careful you don't get a ducking."

I returned no answer to his speech, for I realized that we were losing valuable time, but immediately retraced my steps along the trail we had made, until I reached the rips, and then I started into the river, Spot following me.

Where I first stepped into the water it was only six inches deep, but as I crossed it became deeper, until I stood within about six feet of the opposite bank; the water was clear to the top of my long-legged boots, and I saw that another step forward would fill them.

I did not wish to get wet if I could help it, and I waded up river about a rod, and then down a short distance; but I seemed to have struck a deep channel of some length. As several reasons forbade me spending the rest of the day in dancing up and down the river I made a plunge forward, and reached for a small white birch that grew near the water.

As I stepped forward, the water rose nearly to my shoulders, but I succeeded in seizing hold of the tree, and, after several trials, drew myself out, and then turned to aid the dog, who was making desperate, but unsuccessful, efforts to get on shore himself.

Reaching down, I caught Spot by the collar, and drew him up in the snow beside me. His first performance was to give himself a shake, that spattered my face plentifully with water, and the next to start on a frolic in the snow.

"You rascal!" I exclaimed, "is that the way you pay your master for fishing you out of the river?"

He gave five or six quick, sharp barks, and then jumped up on me, and kissed me, knocking me over as he did so, for I was just pulling off my boots to empty the water out of them.

I picked myself up, and threw a snowball at him, and then, telling him to keep out of the way, succeeded in getting a gallon or two of ice-water out of my boots, and wrung the bottoms of my pants as dry as I could get them. Then I pulled my coat off, and wrung the water out of that as well as I could.

Just as I started for the boat I heard the hoot of an owl floating through the air. Jack had become impatient, and was trying to signal me. I answered him, and kept on.

Ten minutes' walk brought me to the boat, but I could not reach her from the shore. I crept carefully out on the tree, however, and managed to get into her without getting wet again. Spot followed me. I pushed the boat clear of the tree, and, taking my seat at the oars, was soon down to the point where Jack was standing, and took him on board.

"Did you get tired of waiting?" I inquired, as he pushed the boat off, and jumped in.

"Yes," he replied, "I thought you never would come. "Don't you want me to row?"

"Not much. I am wet nearly to my neck, and wish to row to keep warm. I feel half-frozen."

"Did you fall down in the river?" queried Jack, as he made his way to the stern of the boat and took the paddle.

"No; but the water was five feet deep on the other side of the river, and I shall be lucky if I do not take cold from that bath."

"It is too bad you found such deep water; but you will get warm rowing."

As I started the boat fairly on her course again my

teeth began to chatter, and I was seized with a shivering fit. But, after half an hour's rowing, my blood became warmed up, and I felt more comfortable.

We passed a bald eagle sitting on an immense yellow birch that overhung the river, and Jack blazed away at him. The first charge cut away a small limb over the eagle's head into more than a dozen pieces, and the second furrowed the large limb on which the bird sat. He left the limb between the two discharges, and just saved himself " by the skin of his teeth." It was the closest miss I ever saw, and the terrified shriek that the eagle gave when he took to flight showed how badly he was frightened.

We saw quite a number of ducks later on, but did not get a shot at them.

When we reached the lower Metalluc Pond the mist began to clear some, and we caught occasional glimpses of the mountains about us. After running through the Narrows, however, it became thicker, and when we were about five miles from the landing it commenced to snow.

"We started in a snow-storm and shall get back in one," said Jack, disgustedly.

"It does not astonish me any," I replied. "Of all the unlucky trips I ever took this has been the worst. If we get back to Andover alive I shall think we are fortunate."

"This comes of starting on Friday," growled Jack, with a shade of superstition.

"But we did not start on Friday, my boy. Our trip began the morning we left the Upper Dam, and that was Monday."

"But we left Upton Friday."

"True. But our luck was no better before that event than it has been since. If our plans had not miscarried we should not have missed the steamer on Tuesday."

"That's so," replied Jack. "I had forgotten that for the moment;" and he relapsed into silence again.

We found less and less snow the farther down river we went, and when we reached the boat-landing there was not more than half as much as we had left at the lake. The snow that came down now melted as fast as it struck us, and we made haste to get the boat out and take care of her as soon as possible, for we were fast getting wet through.

"Thank God we are so far on our way!" exclaimed Jack, when we had properly cared for the boat.

"Amen!" I added, and pulled on my heavy overcoat, which I thought I could carry easier on my back than in any other way.

Jack picked up the bucket, and put it on the butt of his gun, which he threw over his shoulder. "Let me carry the bucket, Jack," I cried.

"No, I'll take it. I can carry it easy in this way; you have rowed so far you must be tired."

"A lantern would not be a bad thing to have," I suggested, as I glanced around.

"I should say not, and if I ever start on another trip like this I will carry one. You need it as much as you do an axe."

It must have been half-past six when we started down the carry, and only for the snow it would have been darker than coal-tar. That relieved the blackness a little. The wind that had been blowing gently for the last two hours increased its force rapidly, and, as it was in our faces the most of the time, the walk was anything but pleasant. Through the woods the mud was fearful, and I was thankful when we came out in the open pasture, where the walking was a little better.

"Oh for a haven of rest!" I exclaimed, as we trudged wearily along, facing the thickening storm.

"We'll soon reach one if our legs hold out," returned Jack, cheerfully. "But, by gracious, Captain, if we ever go to Parmachenee Lake again I hope we shall have better weather than we have had this time."

"I should hope we would. But I bet five dollars, Jack, that after I get back to Boston you will have nice weather down here for two or three weeks."

"I don't know about that. Any way it does not look much like it now."

"One thing I do know; it will not take me long to find the bed after I eat my supper and get dry."

"I'm with you there, Captain," said my companion.

We arrived at Mr. Fickett's at eight o'clock, and his

wife gave us a nice, hot supper, which we thoroughly appreciated. After drying our clothing we pleaded fatigue to Mr. Fickett, and went to bed, the snow still falling. Our worthy landlord and his wife had been anxious to hear the whole of our story, but I told him I would finish it the next day.

Sometime during the night the wind changed, and the snow stopped its work of powdering mother earth, and when we went out-doors in the morning to have a look at the weather we found we could see the sky, although it was somewhat cloudy and much colder.

After breakfast Mr. Fickett took us down to the Brown Farm, and we amused ourselves there until dinner-time, relating our adventures to a small, but admiring audience. Just as we sat down to dinner we heard the whistle of the steamer, and knew we were all right for our passage down to Upton.

As we arose from the table Capt. Tenney and Chris came in, and, after they had eaten, we all rode down to the boat. Chris told us it was cold and raw out on the lake, and we found it so when the steamer had left the river.

Chris told us there had been a fearful storm during our absence, and asked me where we were the night it blew so. I told him we were in Sunday Pond Camp, and that it had a narrow escape from destruction by a tree falling on it. Jack gave him a history of our trip from the time we had left the steamer until we returned to it, and he was greatly amused, declaring that we had experienced hard luck; in which I fully agreed with him.

As we sat around the open fire in the office of the hotel at Upton that evening, and listened to the accounts of the storm, I again began to feel worried about the safety of our steamer, and told Jack that the boat must have been damaged in that gale.

He tried to laugh the idea out of my head, but it stuck, in spite of his and my own efforts to drive it away.

CHAPTER XI.

*"Who can all sense of others' ills escape
Is but a brute at best in human shape."*—TATE.

BAD NEWS.

AFTER breakfast the next morning, as we could not get any team to take us over, we started to walk to Andover, a distance of seventeen miles. We bade the people in the hotel "good-by," and, shouldering our "collateral," started off at a brisk pace. As we began climbing the long hill that leads to the upper village we were forced to slacken our speed that we might breathe easily.

As we climbed upward we cast an occasional glance back to catch the fine views of the lake presented in the morning sunlight; for the sun had at last condescended to shine once more. There was very little snow on the ground, none to impede our progress but the rough and frozen ground offered poor footing, and I made up my mind that we should be pretty well tired out by the time we reached Andover. As there were no hotels on the way, and we did not intend hurrying, we took a light lunch with us.

When we had reached the top of the hill, and gained a spot which commanded an outlook over the greater part of the lake, we stopped for a moment to admire the beautiful sheet of water below us, now glistening like silver in the sunshine. All the mountains to the northward were covered with snow, and beyond the lake the country had more the appearance of winter than the locality where we were. Having gazed at the beautiful picture before us until we began to feel chilly from standing still we resumed our march.

Just as we passed the road that turned off on the right to Bethel we met one of the Upton guides, who was out with dog and gun on a partridge-hunt.

"Hallo, Captain!" he said; "where are you bound? You haven't started to walk to Boston, I hope."

"Hardly," I replied, laughing. "We are going to Andover, if our courage holds out."

"Did you have any luck up at Parmachenee Lake, hunting?" he asked my companion, with whom he was also acquainted.

"No," replied Jack; "it snowed all the time. We shot at a caribou coming down river, but missed it."

"That's too bad. Caribou is the best meat there is in the woods. Anybody up there now?"

"Three or four when we left. Which way are you going?"

"Down toward Grafton, and I must be moving along. Good-morning."

We returned his salutation, and continued our course over the hills.

From the road where we were now traveling we had a fine view off to the south of Saddleback and Speckled Mountains, the two attendant peaks of Grafton Notch. Each of them was covered with a white cap, but toward their base the snow was very light.

"I don't believe we shall find any snow at Andover," said Jack. "It often snows around Umbagog when we have none over our way, and it seems to me it is getting thinner the farther we get from the lake."

"I don't care to see any more," I returned; "I have had enough to last me for a while."

When we were most down the hill, and near the bridge that crosses the swift Cambridge, Jack saw a hedgehog crossing the road, and fired both barrels at it, killing it as dead as Julius Cæsar.

"Here's something for your dinner, Captain," he cried, as we came up to the animal.

"Thank you; I don't wish to rob you, Jack. Take the game along with you, and you can have some fresh pork."

"I guess not, Captain. That isn't my kind. But I don't suppose I ought to leave it in the middle of the road."

"Of course not. Pitch it into the river. Let me

pull out a few of the quills first; I want some to carry home with me."

"Help yourself."

I took all I wanted, and then, picking Mr. Porcupine up by one of his forepaws, carried him out on the bridge, and dropped him off the lower side. His body struck the water with a splash, and floated down stream till it lodged against a rock.

"That fellow will make good fish-bait," said Jack, watching the dead animal.

"The trout that tries to make a meal on him will get his mouth pricked," I added.

"I don't see what porcupines are good for," remarked Jack, as we began climbing a hill before us about a mile long.

"Years ago the Indians used to take their quills and color them, and use them for ornamenting some parts of their dress; but I don't know of any use they can be put to nowadays, unless the quills might be sold for toothpicks."

"I wonder if they are good to eat, Captain."

"I am sure I don't know. I never knew of anybody eating them; but if I was starving in the woods, and ran across one, I should certainly find out how he tasted. I could not see any sense in your shooting the animal, as he was of no use to us."

"There was no need of shooting him," replied Jack; "but then, you know, it is natural when a fellow has a gun to shoot at everything he sees."

"That is a fact! Man is naturally a most destructive animal."

When we had climbed about half-way up-hill we saw a horse and wagon ahead of us, coming down. It contained two people, a man and woman, but was so far away that we could not tell whether they were old or young; but the horse, even at the distance from which we first sighted the turn-out, seemed skinny and gaunt, and the wagon wabbled along from side to side, with a motion that suggested weak or broken wheels.

We watched the party as they approached us, wondering who they could be, and, as the vehicle came nearer, saw it was about the worst-looking wagon we had ever run across, while the most proper use I could think of for the horse was to tie him up in a cornfield as a scarecrow.

When they had approached sufficiently near for us to trace their faces we saw that the man was old and wrinkled, with huge bushy whiskers, and hair so long that it reached below his coat-collar. His companion was a young girl about eighteen, and decidedly pretty. A slight resemblance in features made me think them father and daughter, and this proved to be the case.

"What a thundering old plug that horse is!" whispered Jack, as we swung to the right, off the road, to be out of the way.

Just as I was about to answer, the horse and the forward wheels became detached from the rest of the wagon, the front end of which dropped down. The hill was so steep in the spot where the accident happened that the hind wheels made a few revolutions, sufficient to land the wagon in the gutter on the left side of the road, while the old man and the girl were pitched out head-first.

As the old fellow went out he turned over, and landed flat on his back, while the girl came down upon him, her head striking his stomach, and then she rolled off all in a heap. It was one of the funniest sights I ever saw, and I could scarcely help laughing, in spite of the possibility of their being badly injured.

The whole affair was over in a couple of seconds, — much quicker than I could tell it, — and Jack and I, dropping our things, rushed to the help of the unfortunates. The horse had gone a few steps and stopped, evidently too tired or lazy to continue farther without urging.

Recalling to mind that well-worn aphorism, "Age before beauty," I knelt down by the old man, although I acknowledge that I should have preferred to tender my services to the young lady, and took a look at him, for as yet he had not moved. I felt of his pulse, and found it to beat fairly strong, and just then he opened his eyes, and made an effort to start up, and with my assistance he gained his feet; but he appeared a little dazed, as if he did not know what he was up to. He seemed able to stand, and I turned to Jack's assistance, who had just called to me, saying the girl had fainted.

A Road Accident.

"Chafe and rub her hands then," I replied, and, having a drinking-cup in my pocket, I filled it with water from a sparkling stream beside the road, and began to sprinkle her face.

Noticing the lower part of her clothing was somewhat disarranged, exposing to our view rather more of a symmetrical pair of lower limbs than her modesty would have allowed had she been in possession of her senses, I told Jack to pull down her dress, which he did just before she came out of her faint, undoubtedly sparing her some blushes.

As she opened her eyes a look of alarm and surprise flitted across her face, until she noticed the old man standing near, and then it changed to wonderment.

"What is the matter?" she asked, trying to rise.

"You have met with an accident," I explained, as Jack and I helped her to stand up.

The old man now found voice for the first time.

"Blast my pictur, if this aint a purty piece o' business!" and he gazed from the wagon to the old horse as if it was too much for him to fathom.

"Do you feel all right, sir, now?" I inquired, turning to him.

"I dunno. I feel kinder shook up in my j'ints;" and then he thought of his daughter, and, looking at her, said, "Are ye hurt any, Bessie?"

"I guess not, father; but how shall we get home? I suppose the wagon is broke."

"I will investigate," I remarked, for as yet none of

us knew the cause of the accident. It had not been the horse, for he was traveling at a snail's pace when the wagon went down.

I went to the body of the wagon and examined the forward part of it, and found that the bolt that secured it to the forward wheels had broken short off, it having been nearly worn out. I was surprised that it had held for any distance at all, in the condition that it was in when they started.

"How far have you traveled this morning?" I asked the old man.

"I came from Blue's, down in the Sarplus; six or seven miles from Andover."

"I don't see how that bolt ever held to draw the wagon up that long hill. It was worn down to a quarter of an inch."

"We walked up all the hills," said Miss Bessie, in explanation.

"Did you? I am surprised that it held even to draw up the empty wagon."

"How am I goin' to fix the durned thing?" inquired the old man. "I live in Colebrook, and wanter git hum to-day."

"The only thing I see for you to do is to go back to the first house, and try and get a piece of iron of some kind, that will answer for a bolt for a short time, and when you get to Upton Village you can get a new bolt made in a few moments, as the road passes a blacksmith's shop there."

"Nobuddy lives in the fust house," replied the old man.

"Try the first inhabited house, then," I replied, laughing. "Any old bolt, or piece of iron rod, that is not too large for the hole, will answer your purpose, if you are careful, until you reach the blacksmith's, and then he can repair the damage properly."

"Which way ye travelin'?" queried the old man, looking from Jack to me.

"We are going to Andover."

"Couldn't ye help me fix this thing? I dunno as I can do it alone."

"I suppose we might;" and I looked at Jack for his opinion.

"Yes, we'll help you," said Jack. "But we need a hammer, and something for a bolt."

"I'll go over and see what I can find at some of the houses beyond, and you can stay here and prevent the horse from running away;" and I winked at Jack.

The old man, who took my remark in earnest, said the horse would not run away, and that he could take care of him.

"All right, I'll leave Jack to help you, then," and I left them.

It was nearly a mile to the second house, the first one, as the old man had said, being empty. I found the farmer who lived on the place out to the barn, and explained to him the nature of my errand.

After submitting me to a cross-examination he remarked that he didn't know whether he had anything suitable or not, but he would look.

He led me from the barn to a small shed, and there he found a box of old iron. We picked this over, and I found a brace that had once done duty on a cart-body, which I told him would answer, and asked him if he would donate it to the cause of suffering humanity.

He stared at me as if he did not exactly comprehend, but finally said: "Yas, you can hev that, mister. What d'ye say the old feller's name was?"

"I didn't say," I replied. "His name may be Smith, Brown, Jones, or Thompson; but as I don't know I can't tell you. Now can you lend me a hammer?"

"Sartainly. The hammer's in the house."

He went in and brought it out, and I thanked him for the iron, and told him I would leave the hammer as I came along, and hurried away before he could question me further.

I returned as quickly as possible, as I did not like the delay we were being subjected to.

When I reached the scene of the accident Jack took the hammer, and after some difficulty succeeded in getting out the upper part of the bolt from the wagon-body. Then, laying our axe on a large flat boulder near at hand, we made it serve as an anvil, and by means of the hammer succeeded in "putting a head" on the old rod I had brought from the farm. Then we hammered the other end down a little, and, trying it on the wagon, found it would work very well.

The old man now backed the horse and forward wheels up to the other part of the vehicle, and we made a connection. With the reins in his hand he walked the horse into the middle of the road, and then told his daughter to "jump in," — a rather difficult feat to execute literally.

Jack helped the young lady into the wagon, and the old man, addressing me, said, " What's the damage?"

"What do you mean?" I inquired.

"Why, what do ye tax me fur your trouble, and fixin' the wagon?"

"Oh!" I exclaimed, comprehending him now, and smiling, I assured him that we had not entered into the speculation from a monetary point of view, but simply to help him out of his scrape.

Jack, with an eye on Miss Bessie, reëchoed my sentiments.

"Wall," remarked the old man, "you're durned accommodatin' young fellers, an' if ye ever cum to Colebrook cum an' see me. I live 'bout a mile this side of the village."

We both accepted the invitation. Passing the reins to his daughter, the old man fished under the seat and drew out a half-gallon stone jug, and, giving it a shake, said : —

"I suppose you fellers take a leetle sumthin' once in

a while, and we'll take a drink all round before we leave."

I caught a pained expression flitting across Miss Bessie's face, and saw that she looked troubled, and like a streak of lightning the idea passed through my brain that she did not want her father to drink. As for me I had never drank intoxicating liquors, and did not propose to begin then. I determined to play a trick on the old fellow, that I felt would have the sympathy of the young lady in the wagon. Taking the jug, I remarked, "I suppose this is the real stuff; here's to our better acquaintance."

I turned the jug up to my mouth; but, just before the liquor reached my lips, my foot slipped on a little piece of ice in the road, and down went the jug, striking against a rock, and was completely demolished.

I cast a swift glance at Miss Bessie, and saw a relieved smile light up her features, and then I exclaimed : —

"Great Scott! But that was too bad. How could I be so careless! My foot slipped on that ice, and, confound it! I'm dry as a fish. I guess I shall have to try brook water now;" and I looked as solemn as the circumstances warranted.

"Wall, don't feel so bad about it; I don't see how you could help it. I was a leetle dry myself, and I can't git anything now till I git to Russell's, and the stuff he keeps is enough to pizen a man."

Don't lay this up against me," I urged, as the old man climbed into the wagon, and took the reins.

"Sartinly not. I don't see how ye could help it. But I must be gittin' along. Good-by to ye."

We shook hands with the old man, as a reasonable excuse for shaking hands with his daughter, and, bidding them farewell, we picked up our things, including the borrowed hammer.

As the old fellow drove off he took one last sniff of the fumes that arose from the demoralized jug, and cast a mournful look at its fragments.

We watched them a few moments, and saw that the wagon was running all right, and then began our upward climb. When we reached a turn of the road, nearly at the top of the hill, which would take us out of their sight, we halted a moment and looked after them.

There was nearly half a mile of space between us, but I saw a white speck fluttering in the air, which I judged to be the young lady's handkerchief, and Jack and I waved our hats in token of recognition. The next moment the white speck had vanished, and Jack and I turned the curve of the road, and that was the last we saw of our chance acquaintances.

We stopped at the house where I had borrowed the hammer, and returned that useful implement. The farmer invited us to stop and have some dinner, saying that it would be ready in half an hour; but as we had already lost nearly two hours, through our unexpected adventure, we declined with thanks, and continued our way.

"That was rather a mean trick of yours, Captain," remarked Jack, with a laugh, — " smashing the old fellow's jug of opedildoc."

"He is better off without it," I returned.

At noon we had passed the last of the houses on East B Hill, and would not see another for the next three miles, this distance being all through thick woods.

On the last upward hill that we had to climb before reaching the Surplus, we stopped a few moments by a little wayside brook, and partook of our luncheon, which we washed down with the sparkling spring-water.

Near the top of this hill we came upon three partridges in the middle of the road, and Jack shot two of them. The cover in the vicinity was very favorable for this fine bird, and if we could have stopped an hour or two we would probably have made a good bag.

I was glad when we had passed the height of land, and began the descent of the long hill that brought us in sight of the Surplus settlement, for we both began to feel tired. As Jack had remarked, the road was nothing but down-hill, and up-hill, and long hills at that. And the miles were like the hills.

An old fellow once told me that the way they measused the miles in that part of the country was to start a fox-hound out at some given point, run him until he dropped dead, and then call it a mile. I give this story for what it is worth, and will not swear to its accuracy.

"Hurrah!" cried Jack, as we swung around the last bend in the hill; "I can see the houses."

When we had reached Dunn's Notch, about seven miles from the village, we met some Andover men, who told us that they had heard the day before that our boat was sunk. A lumberman who had come out from the lakes had brought the news.

Startled and alarmed we asked for particulars, but they could furnish us but a meagre account, adding, however, that the steamer was entirely ruined, and would not be worth the raising.

I did not take much stock in any such report as that, for I knew the boat was thoroughly and substantially built, and would stand a great deal of pounding before being utterly ruined, and telling Jack that we had better get to Andover in the quickest possible time we started at a gait that would have given even a professional pedestrian some trouble to have kept up with us.

"Stories of that kind always grow as they travel," remarked Jack. "I don't believe more than half of it."

"Nor I either. But the sooner we get to the Upper Dam the better, for, no matter what shape the boat is in, she has laid just that way ever since the storm, and we must get her out of the water, if possible, before we have bad weather again."

"I think we shall have two or three good days now," said my companion, glancing upward; "the sky looks hard."

"Present indications are favorable, I acknowledge; but the weather in this country at this time of year is 'mighty onsartin,' as the darky said."

Talking became difficult while we were walking so fast, and we strode on, each amusing himself by his own thoughts, and mine anything but pleasant.

We reached Andover about four o'clock, and found the report verified to a certain extent. We inquired of the landlord of the hotel where we would be likely to find the help we needed, and then went around the village and engaged a crew of men to start with us for the Upper Dam the next morning.

Some people seem to take a malicious pleasure in throwing a man's misfortune in his face, and making it out much worse than it really is. Several of the people whom we met laughed at the idea of our ever getting the steamer afloat again, and told me I had better go home, as it would only be lost time to go to the lake. They were sure that we could do nothing, and seemed bound to make me believe it, if that were possible.

I assured these "wise men of the east" that I should not return to Boston until after I had visited the lakes, and had no idea but what I could get the steamer afloat again, and repair her in such a manner that she would be as good as she was before.

When I thought of what I had seen done to damaged and wrecked vessels at home I almost laughed at the view these fellows took of the accident. I knew, of course, that there were no such facilities for doing the work as there would have been in Boston harbor, but I intended to make brains supply all other deficiencies.

I slept but very little that night, lying awake most of the time, and thinking and planning how to raise the boat and haul her out; but I did not mind the loss of sleep, for excitement took its place, and with the appearance of the first streaks of dawn Thursday morning I arose and went downstairs, and Jack soon followed me.

When I entered the office I found one of the "characters" of the village whom I had not seen the day before. He accosted me with: —

"Good-morning, Cap'n. You've had hard luck with your boat."

"Yes, but I am going up this morning and take her out of the lake."

"Think ye can git her out?"

"I know I can."

"Wall, some of the people 'round here said she was entirely sp'ilt; but I knew better, an' told 'em so."

"There are a great many wise people in this town," I rejoined.

"Yes, wise in their own conceit," remarked the old man, laughing, and then added, "Jack go'in' up with ye?"

"Yes."

"I should like ter go with ye, too, if I wan't so old;

but you'll get her out if 1 du stay ter hum;" and the old man chuckled again.

"Of course we shall."

"Who's goin ter boss the job?"

"I am. But I shall be willing to take advice."

"Shall ye, shall ye? Then ye'll git plenty of it. Every man ye hire'll be loaded with it."

"So much the better, if it's the right kind," I answered.

"Don't ye hav' too many bosses," shaking his head from side to side as he spoke, and holding up the forefinger of his right hand by way of emphasis. "Too many bosses spiles things."

The old man was becoming tiresome, and I was on the point of taking French leave of him, when the breakfast-bell rang, which gave me an excuse for getting out of the room, and I gladly availed myself of it.

CHAPTER XII.

"Down came the storm, and smote amain
　The vessel in its strength;
She shuddered and paused, like a frighted steed,
　Then leaped her cable's length." — LONGFELLOW.

THE WRECKED STEAMER.

WE had an early breakfast, and the men we had hired all put in an appearance at the hotel while we were eating. We were obliged to go to one place and another to pick up tools which I thought would be needed, and it was eight o'clock before we finally gained the lake road and started on our expedition.

On the way to the South Arm various measures were proposed for raising the boat; but, as no one in the party had seen it since the accident, we finally concluded that it was useless to try and make plans until we knew the steamer's condition.

We beguiled the time during our ride with jokes and stories, at some of which I laughed as heartily as any one of the party, for hope had taken the place of fear in my heart, and I thought there was no use in crying for spilled milk.

The road, owing to the recent storm, and the summer's teaming over it, was not in the best condition, and when a wheel would occasionally drop into a mud slough and spatter some unlucky wight it was a signal for merriment. The unfortunate victim received no sympathy whatever.

Occasionally one of the wheels thumped a stone that might easily have been avoided, throwing us out of our seats, and, in one case, nearly throwing us off the buckboard, and then we would blackguard the driver, who only laughed.

Our team was ahead, which gave the driver of the buckboard behind us a chance to chaff our driver whenever he felt inclined, and his calls to our whip "to get out of the road," or "to give him half the road," and "to get out of the way, or he'd run over us," were frequent.

Our driver was abundantly able, however, to keep up his end of the conversation, and the verbal sparring between the two Jehus was quite amusing. Once in a while he would start his horses on a trot, always selecting the roughest part of the road, and his rival was not slow to follow.

"I believe they mean to kill us before we get in there," exclaimed Jack, who sat on the seat beside me.

"I guess we can stand it if they can," I replied," and, besides, it will give us a good appetite for dinner."

We reached the lake at noon, and, after eating our

dinner, launched two boats, and headed for the Upper Dam. The drivers wished us good luck as we left the landing, and, bending to our oars, we were soon out of sight of the teams.

The boats were well manned, and by spelling each other frequently at the oars, we made rapid progress. We raced all the way up the lower lake, sometimes one boat leading, and then the other. The crews were very equally matched, and it was impossible for either boat to keep the lead all the time. This kind of rowing was tiresome, however, and when we reached the lower end of the Narrows the racing stopped, and the boats were pulled along near enough together to allow conversing between the crews.

The lake was very low, and some of the rocks near the channel were out of water. They were well known to Jack and me, for the steamer had been aground on about all of them at different times during the summer, and some of them we had named.

Once or twice we had been out all night, having stuck on a rock on our afternoon trip up, and not getting off till the next day. Our boat was the first steamer that had ever run on the lakes, and drew nearly six feet of water, and this rocky place in the Narrows — the "hop-bed" we sometimes called it — had been a nuisance to us.

There was no chart of either of the lakes over which we had run, and the knowledge the guides possessed as to rocks, sand-bars, and shoals was nearly superficial.

It might do for row-boats, but would not answer for a steamboat. At the close of the season Jack or I, who knew where the rocks were by actual experience, was probably a better pilot than the oldest guide who visited the lakes. The rise and fall of water caused by opening and shutting the gates at the middle dam had also troubled us greatly.

It was a splendid day for our work. The water was as smooth as glass, not a breath of wind stirring, and the air was as mild as in summer. How different from the few days we had passed at Parmachenee!

All of the men were disposed to do their best, and about four o'clock we passed Camp Bellevue, and, skirting the shore, soon came in sight of the steamer, which, instead of being sunk out of sight, as I had supposed from the accounts received about the wreck, lay careened on her port side, in about six feet of water. She had been thrown up quite near the shore on the north side of the river.

The situation was so much better than I had expected that I involuntarily cheered, as I beheld the steamer's position.

Rowing up to her, we climbed over her starboard side, which was all out of water, and began a general survey. The standing-room, engine-room, and cabin were partly filled with water, and we soon discovered that there were two holes in her, but neither of them very large.

"This is not so bad as it might be, Captain," said

THE STEAMER AS WE FOUND HER.

Jack, who was closely inspecting the boat from bow to stern.

"That is a fact. I am glad to find matters no worse."

The lower part of the rudder was unshipped, and had been injured some by pounding against the rocks; but, so far as my observation went, she was not materially damaged, and I felt confident that, if the weather held calm for the next twenty-four hours, I should have her high and dry on land, where she would be safe for the winter, and where by good rights she should have been left in the first place.

The hull of the steamer was very heavily timbered for a boat of her tonnage, and she was planked with southern hard-pine, and thoroughly fastened, and I saw from the way she lay that she could not have been strained much.

Against my better judgment I had been persuaded to leave the boat in the water, the persons who had advised me saying that the steamer would be better off in the water than on shore during the winter, and that the lake never froze where we had anchored the boat. So far as ice was concerned this was all right; but my advisers had not taken into consideration the violent squalls that, rushing down from between the mountains, sweep the lake with terrible force, raising a sea that would be no discredit to a body of salt water. These thoughts passed rapidly through my mind, and I inwardly vowed that this would be the last fall that I would ever leave the steamer in the lake, a prey to the violent winter gales, which are more severe than those of the summer.

Taking Jack with me, I started up the tote road for the Upper Dam Camp, first telling the men to employ themselves to the best advantage they could during our absence.

I found my friend McCard feeling very badly about the accident, and willing to assist me in any way in his power to rescue the steamer from her perilous situation.

He informed me that the gale had been terrible at the Upper Dam, and described the sea as something frightful on the day the steamer went ashore. He said that he had gone down to the lake with some men, but the waves rolled up on the shore so high that they could do nothing. It had been the worst storm around that vicinity that he had experienced for many years.

We spent but a few moments in talking, however, and as soon as the oxen had been yoked to the cart, and blocks, rigging, cant-dogs, axes, pails, and other articles which I thought necessary for the work had been loaded, we started at once for the mouth of the river, where the steamer was lying.

As we bumped along over the road in the ox-cart I laid out my plans, and as soon as we had reached the shore was ready to proceed with the work.

A large hawser was passed over the bow of the steamer, and the bight was worked along under the

THE WRECKED STEAMER. 211

keel, until both ends of the line were opposite the engine-room, and they were then tied together.

The blocks were now carried to a position opposite the engine-room, and one was fastened to a large pine, while the other was made fast to the hawser on the steamer.

The running end of the rigging was next made fast to the ring on the yoke of the oxen, and at a word from me the teamster spoke encouragingly to his oxen, and, bending their heads for the pull, the faithful animals started. As they walked away the rope ran swiftly through the blocks, growing tighter each moment, and soon there was a perceptible strain on the steamer. The driver "Ha Star-ed!" and "Gee Buck-ed!" to his heart's content, the oxen pulled like elephants, and in a few minutes the steamer was brought to an upright position, with her main deck about a foot above water.

Some shores were now set up under her on the starboard side to prevent her careening in shore, and the running line of the blocks was untied from the ox yoke, and made fast to a tree, to prevent the boat going back to her old position.

"Hurrah for our side!" shouted Jack. "That is the way to do it."

"Yes, sir," added Henry W. "We have her now where she can't go back on us."

"We'll have her high and dry by to-morrow," said George R.

"All hands to the pump," sang out Will B. ; "let's get the water out of her."

" I wouldn't begin to pump just yet," remarked Mr. Somes, sarcastically; " I don't think we have crew enough to bail out the lake."

" Who said anything about bailing out the lake?" retorted Will.

" The water will run into her as fast as we can all throw it out, until the leaks are stopped;" and Mr. Somes looked at Will with an exasperating smile.

"I did not think of that," added Will, and a laugh was raised at his expense.

Two of the men now stripped and, going into the hold and cabin of the boat, plugged the holes as well as they could under the circumstances. All hands now began bailing, and in an hour's time had relieved the steamer of water to such an extent that she floated, and we were able to get boards and canvas nailed over the holes so tightly as to nearly stop the leaks in those places.

Then we began bailing again, and kept at it until there were only about ten inches of water in the hold, which did not amount to anything.

" By gracious, Captain ! if this isn't a back-breaking job then I don't know anything," remarked Jack, who was bailing alongside of me.

" It is tiresome work, and no mistake," I returned, as I straightened up to rest my back.

"We have had mighty good luck with the work so far; this water is lowering fast."

"Yes, it is. The only thing that troubles me now is the weather. If to-night and to-morrow are still we shall finish this job all right."

"There is enough of the hard-pine planking left at the Arm to fix those holes, Captain, and I think there were boat-nails enough left also."

"I am glad of it. That part of the job will not be very expensive, as it will not take a man a great while to fit those pieces of plank in."

By this time it was so dark that we could not see to work without lanterns, and as the weather yet had a favorable look we stopped our labors for the night, and went up to the camp, and soon, over a good supper, were congratulating each other on the success already attained.

Many were the hopes expressed that evening that the next day would be calm, for if we could have the lake still until noon by that time we hoped to have the boat out of the water. The last thing I did before retiring was to go out and take a look at the sky, and at ten o'clock the indications were for a still morning, if not a pleasant one.

At seven o'clock Friday morning we were at the lake shore, and dividing the men into two crews; the largest one began work on the ways, under the direction of McCard, while the rest of the men and myself went on board of the steamer.

We found she had only made about four inches of water during the night, which was encouraging, and in a couple of hours' time we had her bailed dry, and then cleaned out some of the ashes and dirt, which had floated through every part of the boat while she lay under water.

"The paint is about spoiled," said Jack, when we had cleaned out the thickest of the dirt. "We can give it a thorough cleaning after we get it out on the ways, and next spring she will need about three coats of paint inside."

"Yes, she'll need thorough painting, and after she is repaired and painted nobody would ever know she was wrecked. She won't show it any when she goes into the water again."

"I wish we had a long chain cable to put around her for the oxen to hitch to. I am afraid our rope will break. There is going to be a fearful strain on it. This boat is awful heavy."

"If it breaks we shall have to mend it and try again."

As the ways on which we were to pull her out were not yet finished, we joined forces with the other crew, and by ten o'clock we had them entirely done.

We had selected the most favorable spot on the shore for the ways, where the land made the most even slope to the water. The ways were built of spruce and fir logs, and were about sixty feet long, extending into the water about eight feet. In construction the logs had been placed about six feet apart; across these ties nearly a foot through were laid, and let into the long logs, or side timbers, to which they were fastened securely with two-inch pins. On top of these ties the bilge timbers were placed. These were the sticks the boat would slide on in coming out of the water, and rest on during the winter, and they had to be hewed very smooth. We had placed poles across the lower ends of the timbers in the water, and weighted them with stones to make the steamer rise easier on the bilge timbers when she left the water.

A large cable was now passed completely around the steamer, going under the wheel and forward of the rudder at the stern, and the two ends were fastened at the bow.

The boat was towed around to the ways, which extended far enough into the water to give a depth of six feet at the outer end. Two poles had been pinned on the centre of the ways to guide the keel, and these ran parallel with the bilge timbers. If we could have built a cradle it would have been much easier, but as we did not have time for that we did the best we could under the circumstances.

The blocks and rigging were now attached to the hawser around the steamer, and, all things being in readiness, the oxen gave a pull. The boat came out of the water thirty feet at the first trial, and this brought the blocks together.

" By gracious, Tom! — that was a good pull," sang

out Will B. as the blocks struck. "It won't take many more like that."

"You're right, it was. I tell you that's a good pair of cattle. But this pull is the easiest. We shall get more dead weight the second pull, and it'll be a miracle if some of the rigging don't break."

"It looks as if the wind was going to blow this afternoon, Captain," remarked George R. to me, and pointing off to the north-west, where the clouds were floating up from behind the mountains.

"Let it blow," I returned. "In an hour it will not trouble us any. This boat will be high and dry in a short time."

"Yes, we'll soon have her out now; we've had mighty good luck over the job, and I'm glad of it."

The oxen were then backed up, and the blocks overhauled for another pull. The second trial was not as successful as the first, for, after the whole weight of the steamer came upon the rigging, the hawser was cut in two by the block hook, and we had to repair damages and try it again.

Before they tried another pull, I climbed on board the steamer and found some old pieces of canvas. These I brought out and wound around the hawser where the hook caught hold of it, so as to prevent it cutting again.

"That is just the thing, Captain," said the teamster; "it will be a great help to the rigging."

Jack had taken the slush-kettle and was putting

more grease on the bilge timbers, so the boat would run easier.

"That is what will make her run easy," remarked Henry W.; "put on plenty of it, Jack."

"You come here, and I'll put some on you, and see if it will make you run easy;" and Jack laughed, as he continued with his labor.

"You can't spare any; you'll need it all for the steamer," retorted Henry.

After three more trials the boat had been hauled out far enough to be safe from ice in the winter, and the high water in the spring, and it was just noon, and consequently dinner-time, when we knocked off work and started for the camp, after giving three rousing cheers for the successful accomplishment of our work. As we were turning away, one of the men descried something swimming across the lake.

We all stopped to see what the animal was. It was heading toward the shore about quarter of a mile above us, and was within perhaps three-quarters of a mile from land when Mr. Somes first saw it.

"It's a loon," laughed Ned R.

"So is your granny a loon," returned Jack, scornfully. "It's not a bird, it's an animal; I should think you could see that if you had any eyes."

"It's a deer," said Horace, who, with his hands doubled up, had been looking at the object through them carefully.

"It's a squirrel, I guess," suggested George R. with

a wink at me. As the animal, whatever it might be, was rapidly decreasing the distance between us, we should soon be able to tell more about it.

We watched it for a few moments longer, keeping up a running fire of remarks all the time, and then Mr. Somes electrified us all by shouting, "It's a bear! it's a bear! — that's what it is, and I say let's go for him, and hurry up, before he gets ashore."

Dinner was no longer an object of interest for us, and all our thoughts centred on the bear. There were no fire-arms among us; but hastily seizing the axes, cant-dogs, and other available weapons, we started for the point where the bear was heading, keeping far enough back in the woods to be out of sight of Bruin, who was making good head-way.

A slight westerly wind had sprung up within the last hour, and this was in our favor, as it blew from the bear toward us, and he would not be so likely to scent us.

It was a go-as-you-please race, and running, jumping, scrambling over large boulders, and forcing our way through a thick growth, we persevered until we were opposite of where the bear was coming out of the water.

We were just in time, and met him at the edge of the woods. It was an old fellow, a he-bear, and one of the largest black bears that I have ever seen. I had only a pick-pole with me, as the other men had taken all the axes and cant-dogs. The bear did not

In Port.

seem to be particularly afraid of the crowd, but stood on all four legs, watching us narrowly.

"Stir him up with your pick-pole," shouted Jack, with a laugh.

Thus advised, I made a jab at his nose, but did not hit him, for the reason that with one blow of his paw he sent my weapon spinning a dozen feet away, and I did not dare to recover it. Then Ned R. made a pass at him with a cant-dog, but Bruin served him exactly as he had me, and knocked it out of his hands. Then he started into the woods.

This was a bad move on Bruin's part, for the crowd was so near him that, as he turned tail to us, the men closed in on him, and gave him some ugly wounds from the rear. With an angry growl he turned and faced us, and, making a sweeping blow with one of his fore-paws, he spoiled Henry W.'s breeches, besides scratching his leg badly. It was funny the way Henry took to the rear; he did not need any help.

"What's your hurry, Henry?" shouted Horace.

"Wait till I tell you," growled Henry.

"Don't you want some pins, Henry?" called Jack, laughing.

"You'll have to go to the tailor's for repairs, Henry," added Ned R.

"I guess I shall need a needle and thread as soon as I get to camp," replied Henry, ruefully, with a glance at his dilapidated pants.

"You had all better let Henry alone," advised Mr.

Somes, "and keep a sharp eye on the bear, or some of you may come out of this fight with something worse than a scratched leg."

"I wish I had a rifle," said Jack.

"Go up to the camp, and get Tom's," suggested Horace.

Bruin now stood up on his hind-legs, and showed his teeth in a manner that suggested business, while Ned and I recovered our weapons.

"Try him with the pick-pole again, Captain," suggested Will B.

"Make an attack on him in front, and I will punch him from behind," I answered.

"We will take up his attention," said George R. and the crowd shouted and threw sticks and stones at him, while I crept carefully behind him. Once in position, I lowered my pick-pole, and made a lunge at him with all my strength, and drove the pick into him a couple of inches. He did not like that fun, however, and he turned towards me, breaking the pole in halves, and made a rush for me. I did not wait to cultivate his acquaintance, and left with all the speed I was capable of making.

Lucky for me, especially in this instance, that I was blessed with long legs, and they were of the kind that would not stand quietly still and see my body abused. In my reckless haste, however, I did not notice much where I was going, and I struck a prostrate tree, that made me go over about as quick as ever I did in my life, and when I picked myself up I had a lump on my forehead about the size of a hen's egg.

A shout of laughter arose from the rest of the party, as they noticed my undignified fall, and three or four jokes were hurled at me, that I felt in no humor to answer.

"Confound the bear!" I muttered, feeling of the bunch on my forehead; "I wish he was on the other side of the lake."

As Bruin turned toward me the crowd pressed in on him and attacked him from behind, and this time the fellows disabled him before he could turn back on them. As Bruin fell to the ground Horace succeeded in striking him in the head with an axe, and after that the men soon killed him. Then some of them cut down a young maple, and Jack ran back to the steamer and found some small rope.

When he returned the bear's legs were tied together, and, running the pole between them lengthway of his body, we took turns in carrying him up to camp. As soon as we reached the house we weighed him, and he pulled down three hundred and fifty pounds.

Before Tom announced his weight there had been a good deal of guessing over it, and the cook had proposed that we make a pool, everybody putting in ten cents, and the one who guessed nearest right to take the money.

A few hesitated at this; but the force of example

was so strong that all hands finally came in but Tom, who did the weighing, and the contributions amounted to one dollar and fifty cents.

I was quite certain that I should not be the one to take the pool, for I was unaccustomed to guessing at the weight of animals, and in fact my guess was the wildest of any one in the party with but one exception.

Henry W. was the lucky fellow, who guessed three hundred and forty-eight pounds, and took the money.

Then all hands took hold and helped to skin and dress the carcass, and Tom cut him up. We had bear-steaks for dinner, supper, and breakfast, for we did not leave until the next morning.

I had ordered the teams to come in after us the second day, and about eight o'clock we started for the Arm, which we reached at half-past eleven, and at four o'clock were in Andover.

I saw Mr. French that night, and arranged to have him go up that winter and repair the steamer, which he did in a most thorough manner, and the next morning I left for Boston. And thus ended my trip from LAKE TO LAKE.

www.ingramcontent.com/pod-product-compliance
Lightning Source LLC
Chambersburg PA
CBHW031824230426
43669CB00009B/1219